Aspects of E. M. Forster

Aspects of E. M. Forster

Essays and Recollections written for
his Ninetieth Birthday 1st January 1969 by

JOHN ARLOTT   ELIZABETH BOWEN   MALCOLM BRADBURY
BENJAMIN BRITTEN   B. W. FAGAN   DAVID GARNETT
K. NATWAR-SINGH   WILLIAM PLOMER   ALEC RANDALL
WILLIAM ROERICK   W. J. H. SPROTT
OLIVER STALLYBRASS (editor)   WILFRED STONE
GEORGE H. THOMSON   PATRICK WILKINSON

 EDWARD ARNOLD

© EDWARD ARNOLD (PUBLISHERS) LTD 1969

First published 1969 by
Edward Arnold (Publishers) Ltd,
41 Maddox Street, London W1
Reprinted 1969

SBN: 7131 5435 7

Printed in Great Britain by
W & J Mackay & Co Ltd, Chatham

Contents

Abbreviations

Page references are to the editions published by Edward Arnold (Pocket Editions where these exist, i.e. AH, GLD, HE, LJ, PI and RV), except for AV (Dent), CSS (Sidgwick & Jackson) and MPI (University Microfilms; see p. 143, footnote 2).

Preface

Elizabeth Bowen tells us that she began reading E. M. Forster in 1915, at a time when his books were hard to obtain. I, too, had this momentous experience in wartime, in 1943 or 1944, with a borrowed copy of *Howards End*. Somehow I had managed to read at least the five novels by October 1944, when I bought Lionel Trilling's critical study, but it was not until 1947, when the Pocket Edition first appeared, that I came to possess any of Forster's own works. Since then I have read and reread his books, lent them to my friends, made new friends through them, and spent hundreds of hours digging for buried Forsterian treasure. (Even a two-line letter to a newspaper can be a tiny jewel.) His writings have given me untold pleasure; his outlook has influenced me more than that of any other writer, living or dead.

Editing this volume, then, has been a work of love and of gratitude, and a joy from beginning to end. The same feelings can confidently be ascribed to the contributors: doubly so to those who are Forster's close personal friends, and whose affection shines out of every page, but also to those who, like myself, know him mainly or solely through his writings, and on whom the nature of their material has imposed a more astringent manner.

My main problem has been one of omission: I started with a list of nearly forty possible contributors, and to whittle this down to fifteen, while preserving a balance between different types of contribution, was no easy matter. One or two people were unable to contribute because of other commitments which would have made it impossible to give of their best in the time available; but there must be many more who would gladly have contributed had they been invited to do so. To all such I can only say that their regret is fully equalled by my own.

Ideally a birthday present should come as a surprise. Any publisher, however, who kept his forthcoming books on the secret list would soon be in Carey Street; and so it was decided at an early stage to tell Forster what was afoot. His friendly interest, and ready permission to quote from his own writings, have been an added encouragement. If he derives from this book a fraction of the pleasure which its writing and publication have given to all concerned, we shall be well content.

O. S.

A Passage to E. M. Forster

by Elizabeth Bowen

There was something to be said for first reading E. M. Forster when I did: 1915. I was then a schoolgirl. In those days, The Novel was not yet a classroom subject. One took notes on Fielding and Richardson, but there it stopped. The copious Victorians had been read aloud to many of us at home, or at school were part of the informality of the drawing-room evenings. In our free time we were, I am glad to say, left to ourselves: our recreational reading of living authors was hit-or-miss—with regard to anything in our own century our likings and judgements were not directed; which was to say, not tampered with. At the boarding-school I was at, a nominal censorship of books brought back after the holidays existed; I recall few collisions with that, and certainly *The Celestial Omnibus* (the 1911 Sidgwick & Jackson edition) met no trouble. Absolutely nothing was known about the author, for or against. The importer, a friend of mine, lent the book round her personal circle. The format itself, fawn-grey binding indented prettily with a gilt pattern, nice-looking thick paper and large print, was promising and beguiling. The contents set up not only an instant enthusiasm but an *engouement*: we were ready to go to any lengths, any expenditure of pocket money, to get hold of more from the same pen. A second-hand copy of *A Room with a View* was procured.

Not long after, I independently had a stroke of luck: investigating a half-empty valise in an attic at the top of an aunt's house, I came upon *Howards End*. Its bedfellows in the valise were, I remember, two books of poetry, Walt Whitman and W. E. Henley. The entombment of these three was, I learned, accounted for by their being relics: they had been the favourite reading of another of my aunts, who was now dead. "Constance," explained her sister, looking at them with feeling as they returned to daylight in my hands, "was very intellectual." However, I was allowed to keep them.

That substantial, scarlet copy of *Howards End* bore the publication date 1910: can it have been, I now wonder, a first edition? After some years, with a then characteristic fecklessness, I lost it. I wonder in whose hands it is now.

The loss, under the circumstances, was catastrophic; it doomed me to remain without *Howards End* for I don't know how long. My passion for Forster novels had, in fact, formed itself during a time when they were increasingly difficult to obtain—the fourteen-year interim between *Howards End* and *A Passage to India*. Owing, one can only suppose, to the novelist's suspension of his activities, and so to a slackening of interest in him, the books for which I thirsted went out of print. The frustration was bitter. The sensation created in 1924 by *A Passage to India* having revived demand for its predecessors, they were reissued, bound to match in aubergine: the Collected Edition.

The lucidity of Forster's writing was, I suppose, what attracted me first of all. Adult fiction had hitherto riled and bothered me by being not only elaborate but, it seemed, fussily enigmatic. It appeared to go out of its way to avoid being straightforward. An Edwardian child, I had given a fair try to such Edwardian novels as came my way, or could be sneaked off tables. All of them had a sort of clique-ish alikeness. I see now, it could have been absence of this which made Forster novels disconcerting to my seniors— who, after all, constituted that vague yet powerful mass, "the reading public". In what other possible way did Forster transgress? The light was too clear, perhaps, the air just too bracing? Or was it that the novels were revolutionary in a manner impossible to pin down? There were few outright aggressions, none of the boldnesses associated with Mr. Wells and Mr. Shaw. Not a single overt hostility met the eye. As story-telling, the story-telling was of an adroitness which confronted no reader with hitch or obstacle. All was—one might have thought—in order.

And why not? For, it is interesting to reflect, the E. M. Forster of all the novels but *A Passage to India* was an Edwardian, and not only chronologically. His work, immaculately turned out, shows the engaging professionalism required in that day. The perfection, or perfectedness, of the novels, qua novels, is wonderfully and civilly inconspicuous: throughout, they are brisk, enticing and shapely. They could appear "light", from their execution being so light-handed. The desideratum for the Edwardian novel was, that it could be read easily and enjoyably. Tension, yes; but let the tension be alleviated by charm and humour. With this, surely, *Where Angels Fear to Tread* (1905), *A Room with a View* (1908), and *Howards End* (1910) comply. *The Longest Journey* (1907) does not; it not so much fails as refuses to; here and there there are affabilities, but the whole is daunting.

I, at any rate, came to *The Celestial Omnibus* with an open mind, the book having no connection with any other, or, for that matter, with anything else. In 1915 one was fortunate in being too young to have formed attachments, for the Great War, opening like a chasm, had swallowed up the immediate past—its tenets, its sayings, its personalities, its *idées reçues*. One was freed from those, at however dreadful a price. Landmarks were swept away, and one did not miss them: they had not been one's own. One began to require those that should be one's own. Where I was concerned, this book became one. The stories within it were revelations—come though they might to be looked back upon, afterwards, as foretastes. Each was a formidable entity on its own. I had had no notion that such things could be done. Few of them, actually, can have attracted me by their subjects: I loathed Pan, for instance, and was inclined to look on the supernatural, other than in the course of a straight ghost story, as fishy. (I liked Miss Beaumont, in "Other Kingdom", however, because she bamboozled a pack of bores, and I ardently took sides with old Mr. Lucas, in "The Road from Colonus", against the dull daughter who cheated him of his fate, while the title story confirmed my feeling for ancient alleys between suburban walls.) No, the magic was not in the matter but in the manner, the telling, the creation of a peculiar, electric climate in which *anything* might happen. In itself, the writing acted on me as an aesthetic shock. There was a blaze of unforeseen possibilities. For instance, the welding of the inexplicable and the banal. . . . At the same time, banality was so treated as to make it appear not only fascinating in itself but absolutely (one might have thought) impervious. With each page, one was in the presence of a growing, not yet definable danger, the blindness of those endangered being part of the spell.

There was a depiction of people in terms not of mockery but of an irony partly holding mockery in curb, partly rendering it superflous. There were types, I noted, to whom the author extended no loving-kindness: they were his targets. The woolly-minded, however fatuous, he let pass; but woe to the complacent, and above all to the culturally-pretentious! *Vide* Mr. Bons in "The Celestial Omnibus":

> Yet even Mr. Bons could only say that the sign-post was a joke—the joke of a person named Shelley.
> "Of course!" cried the mother; "I told you so, dear. That was the name."
> "Had you never heard of Shelley?" asked Mr. Bons.
> "No," said the boy, and hung his head.
> "But is there no Shelley in the house?"
> "Why, yes!" exclaimed the lady, in much agitation. "Dear Mr. Bons, we aren't such Philistines as that. Two at the least. One a wedding present, and the other, smaller print, in one of the spare rooms."
> "I believe we have seven Shelleys," said Mr. Bons, with a slow smile. Then he brushed the cake crumbs off his stomach, and, together with his daughter, rose to go. (css, 39.)

The gruesome death-crash of Mr. Bons is merited: justice is more rather than less inexorable when it is poetic. The wicked are their own executioners, impaling themselves, unaided, on their dooms. . . . Ultimately, though, for me, the central, most powerful magnetism of the *Celestial Omnibus* stories was in their "place-feeling". In each of them action was not only inseparable from its setting but seemed constantly coloured by it and, in one or two cases, even, directly and fatefully set at work by it; and of this there was to be, when I came to the novels, more, much more. E. M. Forster, in his introduction (1947) to the *Collected Short Stories*, admits that two of them—"The Story of a Panic" and "The Road from Colonus"—were inspired by their scenes. "One of my novels," he continues, "*The Longest Journey*, does indeed depend from an encounter with the *genius loci*, but indirectly, complicatedly, not here to be considered. Directly, the *genius loci* has only inspired me thrice." (p. vi.) (The third case was a short story, "The Rock", excluded as an "ill-fated effort".) Intense sense of locality, and deference if not subjection to its power could in itself make distinguishable, did nothing else, the Forster atmosphere. My own tendency to attribute significance to places, or be mesmerised by them even for no knowable reason, then haunted by them, became warranted by its larger reflection in E. M. Forster. Formerly I had feared it might be a malady.

The conversations—in fact, the dialogue of which the stories consisted so very largely—whetted my appetite for more. I had met the like, for lifelikeness, only in *Alice's Adventures in Wonderland*. Here, if there was less diabolical repartee than in the Carroll universe, there was no less effectiveness. One was startled by the extent to which people are characterised by their own words, most of all by those thoughtlessly spoken. How they deliver themselves over to one another by so much as opening their mouths! And the more they do not intend to, the more they do so. That the greater number of speakers of Forster dialogue are either conventional or inarticulate (or both, sometimes) made, for me, their involuntary eloquence more memorable. I learned, also, from these premonitory stories, how great can be the striking-power of the

thing said. Forster talkers are always precipitants of *something*.
When (for the time being) they have done, a situation has changed
for better or worse. Even a random, witless, wandering exclama-
tion or observation has its potentially dangerous edge. Here or
there, the voice of a lover, a rebel, a visionary, a juvenile or a simple person rises out of the trammels of its vocabulary into the
empyrean of poetry. Yet all stays within the bounds of "ordinary"
diction. That seemed to me to be semi-miraculous: I was right, it is.
Untaught, I perceived in Forster the master dialogue-writer of our
century. Variants and experiments continue to run their lively and
harmless course. Basic—because, I imagine, instinctive—knowledge of the "how", not only the "why", of talking remains his.
. . . I look back on *The Celestial Omnibus* as an experience. Outside
poetry, it was my first experience of originality—as such, un-
repeatable. I mean, it could never again be mine with its original
virtue. I do not know when last I reread the stories. They were an
excitement; they were an incitement also.

Of the five Forster novels, the first four burst on the world in a
sort of glorious rush, at a time (1905 to 1910), when I was too
young to know what was going on. As I read them in no particular
order, other than that in which I succeeded in getting hold of them,
chronology plays little or no part in my indelible notion of Forster
novels. As far as I am concerned, they remain phenomena. By
which I do not mean isolated phenomena; their spiritual attachment to one another could not but be evident from the start, as one
by one they entered into my cognisance. That their virtue is, in
the highest sense, communal was not lost on me once I knew them
all. I perceive now what I may not have perceived at first, that
from each one sprang not only the impetus but the necessity for
the one to follow. What was yet to be written would have been
nascent, latent, in what was being written at the time; equally,
what already had been written (or created) was present in what
was being written, adding to the comprehensibility in depth. . . .
I am debarred, as is to be seen, from tracing the "development",

as a novelist, of E. M. Forster, even did I not feel, as I do, that it would be impertinent to attempt to do so. As a matter of fact, I do not believe that novelists do develop: they enlarge. Their area widens; their authority (in some cases) strengthens itself. I say "in some cases" because in that of E. M. Forster this not only was unnecessary but would have been impossible: the author of *Where Angels Fear to Tread* had, already, as much authority as the author of *A Passage to India*.

To revert to the striking-power I first noted in the dialogue in *The Celestial Omnibus*: I saw increasingly, as I came to the novels, how essential it was that the characters be armed—quick on the draw, at the ready. The E. M. Forster majority are more than effectively armed with words. The few who are physically aggressive (Gino, for example, in *Where Angels Fear to Tread*, Charles Wilcox in *Howards End*) are caused to explode into their aggressions by a rising and maddening pressure: their inarticulateness. The world of these novels is a world of conflict; its not being a world actually *in* conflict, fraught by battles and revolutions, makes the schisms within and oppositions between its people stand out more significantly and strongly. As does also, by contrast, the exterior gentleness: dramatically seldom is the surface—ironic, amiable, civilised, mannerly—cracked right across. True, few novels omit conflict, without which they would risk having no plot; simply, in many the conflict seems artificial, or manufactured to serve its purpose, rather than inescapable and inherent. Conflicts in Forster novels are inherent, radically inevitable. They are part of the continuous struggle for integrity. They are part of the way towards understanding: they desire solution. In this aspect the world of the Forster novel cannot but be instantly familiar, commanding and convincing, to a young reader. For me, it had more than verisimilitude; I arrived into it with a sense of homecoming. In this sense, Forster is a novelist for the young. He is no liar. He does not misrepresent.

He was, in fact, young when he wrote these books: twenty-six in 1905, when *Where Angels Fear to Tread* appeared; only five years older when *Howards End* did so; not far into his forties when,

after the interim, came *A Passage to India*. One can now see, from
the vantage point of one's own maturity (as no doubt he does) how
capable he then was of injustices—sweeping, drastic, high-handed,
high-minded youthful injustices. (Is it because he is now just that
we have no more novels?) He is, was, an intemperate novelist;
the intemperance of Dickens, whom I love also, stands out more
conspicuously, but is hardly greater. E. M. Forster is not universally kind to people in the sense that people are taught to be
kind to animals. Some of his leading characters he is drawn to (the
Honeychurch family, all three); some he has a sterling regard for
(Margaret Schlegel); some he cannot prevent himself from ideali-
sing (Stephen Wonham). He would *like* to like; in which he resembles the undergraduate Rickie Elliot. Here, from an early page
of *The Longest Journey*, is an excerpt (cut) from one of those Cambridge conversations:

> "Elliot is in a dangerous state," said Ansell. . . .
> "How's that?" asked Rickie, who had not known he was in
> any state at all. . . .
> "He's trying to like people."
> "Then he's done for," said Widdrington. "He's dead."
> "He's trying to like Hornblower."
> The others gave shrill agonised cries.
> "He wants to bind the college together. He wants to link us
> to the beefy set."
> "I do like Hornblower," he protested. "I don't try."
> "And Hornblower tries to like you."
> "That part doesn't matter."
> "But he does try to like you. He tries not to despise you. It is
> altogether a most public-spirited affair."
> "Tilliard started them," said Widdrington. "Tilliard thinks it
> such a pity the college should be split into sets." . . .
> "The college isn't split," cried Rickie, who got excited on this
> subject with unfailing regularity. "The college is, and has been,
> and always will be, one. What you call the beefy set aren't a set
> at all. They're just the rowing people, and naturally they chiefly
> see each other; but they're always nice to me or to anyone. Of
> course, they think us rather asses, but it's quite in a pleasant way."
> "That's my whole objection," said Ansell. "What right have
> they to think us asses in a pleasant way? Why don't they hate us?

What right has Hornblower to smack me on the back when I've been rude to him?"

"Well, what right have you to be rude to him?"

"Because I hate him. You think it so splendid to hate no one. I tell you it is a crime. You want to love every one equally, and that's worse than impossible—it's wrong. When you denounce sets, you're really trying to destroy friendship."

"I maintain," said Rickie—it was a verb he clung to, in the hope that it would lend stability to what followed—"I maintain that one can like many more people than one supposes."

"And I maintain that you hate many more people than you pretend." (LJ, 26–8.)

Rickie's Cambridge was Forster's: it was, one is reminded, the Cambridge of the Apostles.[1]

But, when it comes to what I spoke of as comprehensibility in depth, the novels go beyond the capacities of youth. They contain more than the still-youthful reader requires, or knows how to look for, or would know how to handle were it come upon. The more often one reads them, and, still more, the later on into life one reads them, the deeper in one goes and the more they mean. These books at once expand and intensify, as does (or should) an individual human life. Did their author, even, originally realise their full content, or how much they involved? It would not shock me to think that he did not—at the time. He himself speaks, in *Aspects of the Novel* (1927), of the prophetic element to be sometimes found in it: the book may anticipate a consciousness yet to be. The Forster novels would seem to belong by nature to a time considerably later than their own (than, that is, the decade in which four of the five were written). They have characteristics which can have only slowly become apparent: they are, for instance, both more primitive and more religious than at first they may have been seen to be. What was once, I gather, known as their "paganism" easily brushes off; not so their physical mysticism.

Love. When is a kiss right, when is it wrong? Look from *A Room with a View* to *Howards End*. Why does George Emerson's kissing of Lucy Honeychurch, on the violet-blue hillside above

[1] See the following essay, p. 17.

Florence, bring about a solution and a redemption, and Paul
Wilcox's kissing of Helen Schlegel, in the summery night of his
father's garden, leave behind it a vacuum, to be filled only by
"telegrams and anger"? Lucy reacts with injury, Helen with rap-
ture; yet it is Helen who is to be the casualty. Both kisses were
impulses—inspirations. Were not both, then, equally innocent?
No; the Wilcox kiss had a tainted source. Falsification of what is
between the sexes, and the possibility of fighting a way out of it,
only just escapes being a Forster obsession. Actively present in all
five novels, it is a constituent of their conflicts. Subsidiary in *A
Passage to India*, it none the less brings about the main crisis: what
did cause Adela Quested's delusion in the Marabar cave, and spark
off the charge she brought against Dr. Aziz? . . . And yet the
thing has its fearsomely funny side. Without it, where would be
Forster comedy? Could one forgo the train journey of the guests
into Shropshire, for Evie Wilcox's wedding?

> The low rich purr of a Great Western express is not the worst
> background for conversation, and the journey passed pleasantly
> enough. Nothing could have exceeded the kindness of the two
> men. They raised windows for some ladies, and lowered them
> for others, they rang the bell for the servant, they identified the
> colleges as the train slipped past Oxford, they caught books or
> bag-purses in the act of tumbling on to the floor. Yet there was
> nothing finicking about their politeness: it had the Public School
> touch, and, though sedulous, was virile. More battles than
> Waterloo have been won on our playing-fields, and Margaret
> bowed to a charm of which she did not wholly approve, and said
> nothing when the Oxford colleges were identified wrongly.
> "Male and female created He them"; the journey to Shrewsbury
> confirmed this questionable statement, and the long glass saloon,
> that moved so easily and felt so comfortable, became a forcing-
> house for the idea of sex. (HE, 221-2.)

"The beefy set?"—cut down to size, polished up a little. It
cannot be said that they transgress; they know nothing of the
battle and the morality. They are without passion. The Forster
élite, his central figures, are people of passion—without exception,
I would say, were it not for *A Passage to India*: Adela, Ronnie,

Fielding are cold fish. But then, there is Aziz. Very often the passions are submerged or muffled; they need to be—they are outlaw passions. They are called upon, also, to bridge gulfs. *Howards End*, the most violent of the novels, surges with them: hostility, pity, sense of injustice, hunger for knowledge are among those rocking the book. The Forster passions are not invariably sexual, or directly sexual. *The Longest Journey* is governed by passions which are not: Stephen Wonham's passion is for the earth on whose breast he sleeps at the very end of the novel. Stephen, the bastard half-brother, the doltish child of "poetry and revolution", at once complements Rickie and assuages him.

Above the battle, guardians of morality, are the elderly women. They have a Fate-like quality: Mrs. Honeychurch, Mrs. Wilcox, Mrs. Moore. . . . Satanic Mrs. Failing and operative Mrs. Herriton rank just less highly. The great three are not only creatures of temperament but inject a further degree of temperament into the books they severally inhabit; two continue to do so after their deaths (Mrs. Honeychurch, fortunately, survives). They are capricious; they unaccountably veil themselves in huffiness. They are Nature. One passes directly on from them into weather and landscape. "Landscape"?—I mean, the formidable, ever-amazing shapes of pieces of country. The concern is with what these shapes give off, what they do to man. What do they not? They impart the sense of existence, of how ancient it can be, how volcanic it can be, and of how it continues. These are, therefore, the dominants in the novels—all the novels, not only *The Longest Journey* in its Wiltshire part. England, Italy, India, unalike, fascinating the pen as they do the eye by their singularities, have in common an underlying, impenetrable strangeness. In his unceasing awareness and awe of this resides, for me, no small part of the genius of E. M. Forster.

This piece of mine, called "A Passage to E. M. Forster", strikes me, now that I near the end of it, as having had no particular bourne. I accepted the title, tentatively suggested by the book's editor, with no intention, or hope, of ever really converging upon the author. Who am I that I should? Neither do these pages qualify either as an appreciation or as a tribute. I have written, rather, a sort of autobiography: the autobiography of an E. M. Forster reader. And when I say E. M. Forster, I mean the novelist, who was also the donor of the short stories. Some sort of recalcitrance makes me blind to him in any other capacity. Even within the bounds I have set myself, I should have done better than I have; I am aware of having been scrappy, arbitrary, over-impressionistic. I could be the first to point out glaring omissions. What, for instance, about the great part music plays in the novels? (The fact is that I am not musical.) Why have I referred less constantly, and more sketchily, to *A Passage to India* than to its fellows? I suppose because I resent its having stolen the thunder from them. But after all, autobiography is accorded the right to be disproportionate, prejudiced, and subjective. The main thing is that I am so saturated in the writing (the novel- and story-telling) of E. M. Forster that I find it hard to look on either the works or the author behind them objectively. I can think, also, of no English novelist who has influenced me more.

How lucky I am that it was he who did. It seems to me impossible for a writer, at his or her outset, not to be influenced. (Though, for the matter of that, who influenced *him*? One finds no traces.) I was reading him, and addictively, for some years before I thought of writing myself. (In those years I thought I was going to be a painter.) When I did begin, I do not mean that I copied him. More, he considerably affected my view of life, and, as I was to discover, my *way* of writing. For this influence I feel unqualified gratitude; without it, I should not even be what I am. I should like to close, however, by recording the joy he has given me, and by saying, I now see how this came about. In his 1925 Hogarth Press essay *Anonymity*, he says that when reading "The Ancient Mariner": "We have entered a universe that only answers to its own laws, supports itself, internally coheres, and has a new standard of truth." This is so, and has always been so, for me each time I enter a Forster novel.

Forster and King's

by Patrick Wilkinson

Some years ago the editors of a miscellany by Old Tonbridgeans approached E. M. Forster for a contribution. He replied offering to write on "How I got out of playing games at Tonbridge". The offer was not taken up. He had, in fact, been allowed by his headmaster to go for bicycle rides instead, which suggests an elasticity not generally credited to public schools of that period. One can hardly conceive, however, that any public school could have been warm and imaginative enough for the shy and sensitive boy whose father had died before he could remember him, and who was being brought up by his mother and maiden aunts. He was not made of such stern stuff as another day-boy who entered Tonbridge in the same term, the future Field-Marshal Lord Ironside of Archangel, and going home to shelter at night may have served only to intensify the cold winds of school. However, his bitter memories of Tonbridge, the "Sawston" of *The Longest Journey*, were due less to treatment of him as an individual than to a shrinking from the whole ethos of the place. He escaped in 1897.

In that year he went on to King's College, Cambridge, chosen for the next stage in his education. His father had been at Trinity, but its large numbers and reputation for boisterousness may have made it seem unsuitable. King's was certainly the right college for him. "The college, though small, was civilised, and proud of its civilisation. It was not sufficient glory to be a Blue there, nor an additional glory to get drunk." So he wrote not many years later, in *The Longest Journey* (pp. 68–9). The characteristics of Tonbridge which had alienated him were not conspicuous there, though they did persist in Cambridge in the heartier circles he once grouped together under the term "the varsity" (GLD, 104). When King's, nearly fifty years before, had given up its so-called privilege and had begun to take the University's examinations for degrees, it had decided that all its members should read for Honours. Again, it already had a tradition, perhaps derived from Eton, of easy association between junior and senior members, in the fostering of which, to do him justice, Oscar Browning played a considerable part.[1] "The direction of the swim" (to continue the quotation) "was determined a little by the genius of the place—for places have a genius, though the less we talk about it the better—and a good deal by the tutors and resident fellows, who treated with rare dexterity the products that came up yearly from the public schools. They taught the perky boy that he was not everything, and the limp boy that he might be something. They even welcomed those boys who were neither limp nor perky, but odd—those boys who had never been at a public school at all, and such do not find a welcome everywhere. And they did everything with ease—one might almost say with nonchalance—so that the boys noticed nothing and received education, often for the first time in their lives." (GLD, 69.)

The contrast with school was an exhilarating liberation; and more positively it was an inspiration due not so much to the glory

---

[1] Oscar Browning was a baroque figure, who had been an educative force as a master at Eton. Dismissed by the headmaster, Dr. Hornby—unjustly, as many considered—he continued his activities as a Fellow of King's. He was always in debt, and was an absurd snob; but he broke down barriers, blew away stuffiness, and though something of a charlatan introduced young men to the pleasures of literature and music, and encouraged them to believe in themselves. There is a good biography by his nephew, H. E. Wortham: *Oscar Browning* (Constable, London, 1927).

of the Chapel, so overwhelming to some as to make it seem almost alien, as to the open beauty of the Backs, and to the associations of the place, echoing to wave after wave of youth and discourse over the centuries. "The Cephissus flows with the Cam through this city, by the great lawn of King's under the bridge of Clare, towards plane trees which have turned into the chestnuts of Jesus. Ancient and modern unite through the magic of youth." (GLD, 103.)

"The Cephissus" is a reminder of what Forster had come to study. It was Classics, and this had the incidental merit of bringing him immediately into close relationship with a great educator, one of the most stimulating influences in the College, Nathaniel Wedd, then aged thirty-three. Wedd, who was as yet unmarried, is unknown to history save from books about or by Forster. This is partly because he was incapacitated by illness for ten years in the middle of his life and later by periods of eye trouble, but also because he was indifferent to fame and considered helping and teaching the young more important than "producing", though Lowes Dickinson described him as "one of the ablest men I have ever known". Lord Birkett, who had been at Emmanuel, when speaking at King's Founder's Feast in 1960, recalled across the years the excitement of Wedd's lectures on Greek History. I knew him as a teacher and colleague in his last fifteen years, marvelled at his verbal memory, and envied him the immediate contact he established with pupils, so that what had begun as a Latin prose supervision might end with the pupil confiding to this septuagenarian the intimacies of his life, his family, his love affairs, his hopes and fears. Coming up from City of London School, he had been, with his lifelong friend J. J. Withers, a protagonist in the feud of his undergraduate days against the arrogance of the self-styled "Best Set", whose arbiter was A. C. Benson and whose criterion was "good form". He was small but dynamic, irreverent and all his life instinctively against authority, whether secular or ecclesiastical, cynical and ironical in a most amusing and heart-warming way, yet a passionate champion of what he believed to matter. As an undergraduate he had secured the subversive

Bernard Shaw to speak to a College society, and as a don he ensured that the works of Ibsen, Zola, and George Moore were added to the College Library.

It is widely believed, owing to the admiration and affection that permeate Forster's full-length biography of Goldsworthy Lowes Dickinson, that "Goldie" was the formative influence on him. But he himself has always insisted that it was Wedd. "It is to him . . . more than to anyone that I owe such awakening as has befallen me." (GLD, 73.) In fact, though he did know Dickinson as an undergraduate,[2] it was chiefly in his fourth year that he became a devotee, and then not as a pupil (Oscar Browning unfortunately barged in there) but as a member of the Discussion Society Dickinson had founded for like-minded undergraduates from all colleges. The long years of intimacy came later. It was Wedd who encouraged him to write; and amid the accumulation of papers he left at his death was found an early version of *Where Angels Fear to Tread*, now in the College Library, together with a novel by himself, nearly completed, on "the new woman".

What Forster got from his classical studies is rather intangible. He recalls with amusement the howls of pain that a false quantity would wring from teachers of verse composition at school. Six years after he left Cambridge Dickinson procured for him the assignment of contributing an introduction and notes to E. Fairfax Taylor's translation of the *Aeneid* in the Temple Classics. (His introduction was recently reprinted in Everyman's Library to accompany Michael Oakley's translation.) One might not have expected the poet of Rome's imperial greatness to appeal to him, but his assessment is very fair: "At the present day poems are not written thus, and the modern reader sometimes wonders why a poem that is patriotic rather than human should have held humanity so long. One reason, perhaps, is that we can read the *Aeneid* as patriots.

[2] In April 1898, prompted by a common acquaintance of their families, Dickinson asked the freshman to a tête-à-tête lunch. They had "Winchester cutlets, a sort of elongated rissole to which he was then addicted" (GLD, 100). I cannot forbear to add that it was at lunch with Dickinson some thirty-three years later that I first met Forster. We had Winchester cutlets.

Our civilisation comes from Rome, and it concerns us personally that she once became great." (AV, viii.) His dislike of Augustus as a man is more characteristic, and was not at all common then.

But we should expect Greece to appeal to him more. We may presume that he had read Dickinson's *The Greek View of Life*, that distillation of what was fine and unique in ancient Greece, which appeared just before he came up, and which has captivated generations of readers, and still does, though nowadays it is criticised for inattention to the seamy side. But we may suspect that the Mediterranean setting and mythological symbolism of one or two of his short stories was suggested less by his classical studies—years later he sighed over an American Ph.D. candidate: "He has come all this way to connect me with Aeschylus"—than by a visit to Greece in 1902 (a year after he left Cambridge), which was made possible by a gift of £50 from an old lady. After being placed in the Second Class in the Classical Tripos of 1900 and nevertheless, significantly, awarded an exhibition by the College, he diverted to history for an extra year and got a Second in that as well; but reading essays to an Oscar Browning sitting back somnolently with a red handkerchief over his face was no substitute for Wedd, and no consolation for not being entrusted, as he would otherwise have been, to Dickinson.

Wedd was a member of the Apostles, the Cambridge discussion society founded about 1820, membership of which is supposed to be secret during a man's lifetime; but only undergraduates, apparently, take part in elections, and it was H. O. Meredith who sponsored this diffident freshman, "the elusive colt of a dark horse"[3] as Keynes was to call him even when he had made his mark. Thus was opened the way to friendship beyond King's with some of the finest spirits of Cambridge, both present and past (for non-resident members continue to belong). But our best sources for his undergraduate experience are retrospective. It is reflected from close up in *The Longest Journey* (begun some time before its publication in 1907), whose hero Rickie Elliot contains a great deal of himself. (This is the most spontaneous of his novels, and

[3] J. M. Keynes, *Two Memoirs* (Hart-Davis, London, 1949), p. 81.

the one he says he is most glad to have written.[4] It is also recaptured at a distance of thirty-three years in his life of Lowes Dickinson.

In Bodley's neo-gothic, L-shaped building beside the river at King's there is a room—W7 to be exact—which is exceptional in having a board recording the names of all the occupants since the building was completed in 1893. (I am familiar with this, since the room was my home from 1927 to 1930.) One of the earliest names is E. M. Forster. The narrow bedroom window has a glorious view southward over Queens' garden to the timbered Tudor Lodge of their President; the sitting-room looks north to King's and Clare bridges. (Where G. L. Kennedy's extension now intrudes there were elm trees then.) It is on the top floor, so that no one drops in who does not really want to see you. This—despite the decoy words, "Last night the bedmaker from W said to me" (LJ, 15)—must be in imagination the room in which Rickie and his friends were discussing in the firelight whether or not the cow was really there when Agnes Pembroke burst in and turned on the electric light. Ansell, his closest friend, was modelled on Alfred Ainsworth, a brilliant scholar, who got two Firsts in Classics and one in Moral Sciences, an Apostle, a leader in the intellectual world of King's and Trinity, a devotee already, before the publication in 1903 of *Principia Ethica*, of the philosopher G. E. Moore (whose sister he was later to marry). In real life he was, like Ansell, "ardent, high-minded, sincere and argumentative".[5]

Hardly any contemporary now survives. One can only go by what one has heard from Forster himself, or from others in the past, or read. And this is what we read of Rickie: "He had crept cold and friendless and ignorant out of a great public school, preparing for a silent and solitary journey, and praying as a highest favour that he might be left alone. Cambridge had not answered his prayer. She had taken and soothed him, and warmed him, and had laughed at him a little, saying that he must not be so tragic yet

[4] World's Classics edition, Oxford University Press, London, 1960, p. ix.
[5] Obituary in the privately circulated *King's College Annual Report* for 1961, p. 64. After four years as a Lecturer in Greek at Edinburgh he joined the Board of Education, and ended as Deputy Secretary.

awhile, for his boyhood had been but a dusty corridor that led to the spacious halls of youth." (LJ, 10.)

As Rickie lay with his friends in a meadow during their last summer term he sighed: "Cambridge is wonderful, but—but it's so tiny. You have no idea—at least, I think you have no idea—how the great world looks down on it." Ansell pounces on him. There is no such thing as "the great world"—only tiny societies, some good, some bad (pp. 73-4). I remember hearing of a similar scene forty years later. A Scottish ex-miner had come up to King's for interview. An undergraduate, a miner's son (already, incidentally, a friend of Forster's) was asked to look after him, and friends of his came in for coffee after they had dined in hall. The usual sort of discussion arose, and when he could get a word in edgeways the visitor interposed: "You know, you people are a very long way from the real world." They pounced on him just as Ansell might have done, though perhaps more gently: "Oh, no: *this* is the real world." Forster himself once wrote of King's: "In its exquisite enclosure a false idea can be gained of enclosures outside, though not of the eternal verities." (GLD, 104.) It is sometimes said that universities ought not to be situated in paradises, but among the people who, in sordid surroundings, do the work that ultimately sustains them. There is obviously some force in this argument. But is it not equally important that there should be scattered throughout the country in all classes people who have had a vision of what ideally life might be like? They may find the contrast distressing at times, but like Plato's philosophers they must go back into the Cave.

It was Lowes Dickinson, I suspect, who enabled Forster to understand in retrospect what it was that he owed to King's and to Cambridge. An irritation with Dickinson as a man and as a writer, however persuasively supported by documentation, is to my mind the only serious flaw in Wilfred Stone's admirably sympathetic and penetrating study of Forster, [6] to which indeed I

[6] Wilfred Stone, *The Cave and the Mountain: A Study of E. M. Forster* (Stanford University Press and Oxford University Press, Stanford and London, 1966).

am much indebted. I knew him only in his last years; but I recognise at once the lighting up of the face which Forster said he observed as a freshman when he nervously admitted that he did not think a play he had asked Dickinson to lend him was very good (GLD, 100). We regarded him as a sort of touchstone of sincerity. He was a Socratic genius, and the incarnation of those discussion societies that have educated undergraduates more than any tutorials. When some of us in my year in College started one, he was the first guest we invited; and a group in the next year named after him the one they in turn founded, which was to go on meeting in London even after they had gone down.

Of such societies Forster has written:

> The young men seek truth rather than victory, they are willing to abjure an opinion when it is proved untenable, they do not try to score off one another, they do not feel diffidence too high a price to pay for integrity; and according to some observers that is why Cambridge has played, comparatively speaking, so small a part in the control of world affairs[7] . . . Their influence, when it goes wrong, leads to self-consciousness and superciliousness; when it goes right, the mind is sharpened, the judgement is strengthened, and the heart becomes less selfish. There is nothing specially academic about them, they exist in other places where intelligent youths are allowed to gather together unregimented, but in Cambridge they seem to generate a peculiar clean white light of their own, which can remain serviceable right on into middle age. (GLD, 66.)

This applies to the Apostles, in so far as it is not an idealisation, as much as to the people Forster knew at King's. Rickie wished that such people could go through life somehow labelled (LJ, 75), so that they could recognise one another.

[7] I think this applies to Cambridge since G. E. Moore, as compared with Oxford since Jowett; not to the old Cambridge that bred the Elizabethan Cecils and Walsingham, Bacon, Strafford, Cromwell, Walpole, Pitt, Castlereagh. Keynes is an exception, as having been very much nurtured among the Apostles; and his activities on the world stage were regarded with some suspicion by his Bloomsbury friends.

Does this all seem rather priggish? Inevitably, perhaps. In the first place, such things cannot be put into words without distortion and overstatement. And again, it is hardly possible for privileged people, an "in-group", to expect an unprejudiced audience when they talk about what they feel and do, especially when, as the Apostles did, they divide others into the "saved" and the "not-saved". But that does not necessarily mean that what they say is untrue.

I must now pass over forty years during which Forster, aided at first by a legacy from his great-aunt Marianne Thornton, established his reputation as a writer. He retained, of course, many links with the College. Some were direct, through Fellows who were friends. There was always Dickinson, but there were also three contemporaries who were awarded Fellowships for six years soon after graduation. The first was E. J. Dent, later to achieve international reputation as a musicologist and to return to the College as a Professorial Fellow. His friendship with Forster is a little surprising, for although their views coincided in many ways, and Dent's conversation about music must have been fascinating to him, there was a certain acidity about him which one does not associate with Forster. However, four months after he had gone down we find him telling Wedd in a letter[8] that Dent is his chief Cambridge correspondent. It was written from the Pensione Simi in the Lung'Arno delle Grazie at Florence, where the ideas for *A Room with a View* were germinating; and Philip Herriton in *Where Angels Fear to Tread*, in so far as he does not represent the author, is modelled on Dent, who knew this and "took an interest in his own progress".[9] Indeed, it was he who suggested the title.

The second, an exact contemporary, was the wise Hugh Meredith, that remarkable character who was to combine being Professor of Economics at Belfast with a lasting passion for Greek

[8] Quoted by Stone, *op. cit.*, pp. 401–2.
[9] "The Art of Fiction: I, E. M. Forster", *Paris Review*, I (1953), 37.

drama. (In the period of trade depression between the two wars he once produced an English version of Sophocles's *Philoctetes* with a cast of unemployed dockers.) And the third was the scientist George Barger, later Professor of Chemistry at Edinburgh.

An older non-resident Kingsman (also, incidentally, a graduate in science) who became a great friend was the art critic Roger Fry, later an Honorary Fellow of King's and for three years Slade Professor at Cambridge. Fry was an Apostle, and Forster also got to know, as an occasional visitor to the Bloomsbury Group, a King's Apostle younger than himself, Maynard Keynes, but not so well as, for instance, W. J. H. ("Jack") Sprott, eighteen years his junior, who became Professor first of Philosophy and later of Psychology at Nottingham and has remained a lifelong friend.

But keeping in touch through friends was not the same thing as residence; and even when the College elected him a Supernumerary Fellow from 1927 to 1933 (Trinity had appointed him Clark Lecturer for 1927) Forster did not reside. His mother was then still living at Abinger Hammer in Surrey, and for most of the time he lived with her. But she died in 1945, and when, shortly afterwards, he was elected an Honorary Fellow someone (George Rylands, I think) had the excellent idea that he should, as an exception, be invited to reside. There was some hesitation about how complete the residence should be, but an easy compromise presented itself. It so happened that my wife and I had recently taken a small house, 3 Trumpington Street, a little beyond Addenbrooke's Hospital, and we had two modest rooms to spare. So for the next seven years Morgan (as I cannot but call him from now on) became our lodger, sleeping and hiding there, and going into College generally before lunch, to return after dinner. From his own point of view it was something to have a refuge from the flattering but exhausting attentions of the "Forster industry", which was gathering momentum both at home and abroad. In College he inherited, most appropriately, a large study on Staircase A in Wilkins's neo-gothic building, facing south on to Chetwynd Court, in the very set which Wedd had occupied during the last decades of his life until his death in 1940. (After we moved, in 1953, he was assigned a bedroom on the same floor in College.) A heavy marble mantelpiece was removed, and the open fireplace was now framed instead by a tall and broad wooden structure composed of shelves and pigeon-holes for ornaments, plain and rather elegant, which had been carved by his father the architect. The room soon took on the character of its occupant, filling up with possessions valued, some for their beauty, some for their associations. The furniture appears to have gathered round him, not to have been deliberately chosen. There is a general air of Victorian sensitivity which is yet far from what was normal in his undergraduate days, when rooms tended to be decorated by the College in a colour known as "Bursar's Bile". In the middle stands the oval walnut dining-table from Battersea Rise, described on page 17 of *Marianne Thornton*, which was from the end of the eighteenth century the nursery table of the family.

Thus began a new life for him at the age of sixty-six, perhaps unimagined by the reading public. At Founder's Feast in 1952, replying to the toast of "The College", he confided to the proposer, Lord Cohen: "I have to tell you that I do not belong here at all. I do nothing here whatsoever. I hold no College office; I attend no committee; I sit on no body, however solid, not even on the Annual Congregation; I co-opt not, neither am I co-opted; I teach not, neither do I think, and even the glory in which I am now arrayed was borrowed from another College for the occasion." But though he had no regular pupils he got to know without apparent effort a very large number of undergraduates, and was able to be to them, in a College now almost denuded of bachelor dons, what the young Wedd and Dickinson had been to him. It must have seemed to him both an opportunity to repay, and, in a sense, a return home, deeply though he felt the loss of West Hackhurst at Abinger, where he had lived for many years. Naturally his fame was a help, acting as a kind of introduction; and just how famous he had become was brought home by such things as an invitation to represent European literature at the tercentenary of Columbia University along with Thomas Mann

and André Gide;[10] but he would have got to know the young in
any case, because he was so approachable and himself took every
opportunity. During the earlier years I was Senior Tutor of the
College, and when we had students in for drinks before lunch on
Sundays he generally joined us. There was one unavoidable
hazard: as often as not an introduction was a cue for "Please, Mr.
Forster, why haven't you written a novel for so long?" But he
invariably answered without a flicker of impatience—usually with
some variation of "Well, I hadn't anything more I wanted to
say."

He was invited to join the Ten Club, originally a play-reading
society but recently more varied in its activities, and in his
eighty-ninth year still took his turn at entertaining it, on an evening when members read aloud poems of their choice. But still
more he has time for individuals. At the theatre or a concert he
is very often accompanied by an undergraduate, and seldom by
more than one. One undergraduate whom I asked whether he
knew him replied: "Oh yes: when I was a freshman he used to
come to tea with me once a week." Those who are shy or less fortunate in some way particularly attract his interest, the Rickies of today, and those from other countries, especially from the East. But
his manner of approach is diffident: he does not assume that an advance will be welcome, however often he must have found it to
be. And everyone is treated with the same courtesy. Naturally he
does not always agree with modern ideas, but he listens and turns
them over, not rejecting them out of hand. Any idea could be
important that comes from first-hand experience. Of Dickinson
he wrote: "By the end of his life he had become so wise that he

---

[10] Misapprehensions, however, occasionally arise. A young American
dining as a guest in Hall was introduced, and delightedly claimed to
have read all his books. Asked up to his rooms afterwards, he listened
for some time to unexpected topics of conversation, and finally interposed: "If you are so keen on music, why did you make Captain Hornblower tone-deaf?" Hearing him hailed by someone as "Morgan" at a
London party, an effusive woman hurried over: "Are you Charles
Morgan?" "No, I'm Morgan Forster." "Oh, I'm so sorry: I thought
you were the writer."

was able to learn from the young." (GLD, 102.) The same might be said of himself. And all this has gone on now for more than twenty years, enhancing the life of the College in general and of countless individuals for whom it may well be their most treasured memory of Cambridge. Of course, age and increasing difficulty in remembering names and faces has reduced it; but there is still the staircase, that cell of Cambridge social life; and the establishment in 1967 of a Common Room with a bar, which can be used by the entire College, and which happens to lie between his rooms and the hall, has given him a chance to pick up a glass of wine on his way to dinner and join some group of undergraduates. His many clandestine generosities I must mention, but may not specify. I might add here that no Fellow, let alone an octogenarian, can ever have been more conscious of the College staff as human beings, more considerate and courteous to them. And he endured with incredible good-humour the upsets occasioned by the major building operations round and under his rooms that took place in his eighty-ninth year, not even complaining about the architecture, which could hardly please him—not to mention visits from lion-hunters, or the occasion when he found six French girls giggling in his bathroom. His only protection has been not having a telephone.

Naturally he has had many friends among senior members also: one source of happiness to him in his eighties, for example, was the tenancy for a time of the neighbouring rooms, the other half of Wedd's set, by Jayant Narlikar, the brilliant young Indian mathematician who collaborates with Professor Fred Hoyle. But as he wrote again of Dickinson, "for him the undergraduate is the true owner of the University, and the dons exist for the purpose of inducting him into his kingdom." (GLD, 103.) In that speech in 1952 at Founder's Feast, which is attended by all undergraduates in their third (now generally final) year, he took as his theme "Who owns the College?" He cheerfully explained why it was not the Governing Body, nor the Provost, nor the Bursar, nor even that impressive figure the Praelector, though "when he advances up the Senate House with four men hanging from his fingers like

fish, when with a generous gesture he unhooks them and drops
them at the Vice-Chancellor's feet, he seems omnipotent." He
concluded that it was the Third Year; and further, that the College
consisted of all the Third Years there had ever been. "In my first
year I wasn't sure of my clothes. In my second year I was too sure
of myself. In my third year I was just right. Without arrogance
and with exultation, with occasional song and dance, I owned the
place. . . . I knew that other Third-Year men had felt the same,
and would feel the same in future; and I knew—this is significant
—that my kingdom would not last long. And it didn't. I lost my
Kingdom of King's when I took my B.A. degree and became a
graduate of the University, and it has never returned. But something remained: loyalty remained—in fact this is the only un-
forced loyalty I have ever experienced."

The remarkable musicality and musical knowledge of so many
students today has provided him with much common ground. He
has been a constant attendant at the College concerts which take
place on Sunday evenings about four times a term. On 1 March
1959, in honour of his eightieth birthday two months before, the
Musical Society put on one for which he was invited to choose
the programme, subject to the availability of talent. It was as
follows:

Overture: Coriolan	Beethoven
Variations Symphoniques for piano and orchestra	Franck
Lieder:	
(a) *Dämmerung senkte sich von Oben*	Brahms
(b) *Anakreons Grab*	Wolf
(c) *Zueignung*	R. Strauss
(d) *Allerseelen*	R. Strauss
Trumpet Concerto in E flat	Haydn

No one would call him a committee man, and what he confessed
about his anomalous position in the College was practically true.
He did, however, serve on the Garden Committee for a time,
though apt, it was said, to be distracted from its deliberations by

looking at the flowers. (Actually he thought the King's garden fell between the two stools of grandeur and domesticity, preferring the closely planted intimacy of that of Clare, which was no further away.) In the division of opinion as to whether the chaste proportions of Gibbs's Building should be blurred, if embellished, by window-boxes he was on the side of the romantics.

With his Wedd-like suspicion of authority he tended to refer to what would now be called "the Establishment" as "they", even when speaking to me, a member of it *ex officio* at the time. But in due course he was invited to attend meetings of the Governing Body, though the statutes preclude an Honorary Fellow from voting. He has seldom spoken, and has been most effective, perhaps, on occasions when, being unable to be present, he has sent a letter to be read out from the chair. I wish I could quote verbatim the one he wrote when a proposal for enlarging our student numbers was on the agenda. It was to the effect that, whereas in business generally expansion might be beneficial it was harmful to *our* business, which was to produce civilised people.

As for Cambridge at large, he has for some years been President of the Humanists. He is a constant supporter of the Arts Theatre, and a generous donor to the Fitzwilliam Museum. He likes the surroundings, too—the sudden moment on the Barton Road when you can see the countryside ahead and look back at the towers and pinnacles of the city, and Wandlebury on the Gog Magog Hills, to whose preservation he contributed, with its great trees.

On 9 January 1959, to celebrate his recent eightieth birthday, the Provost and Fellows gave a luncheon which was something of a literary occasion. I have the table plan before me now. On his right sits Charles Mauron, the blind Mayor of St. Remy who introduced his works to France; and near him on the opposite side is George Seferiades, the Greek poet "Seferis", then Ambassador in London. I see the name of Edith Oliver of the *New Yorker*, and those of two American actors devoted to him, Bill Roerick and Tom Coley. There are authors here who are among his closest friends—William Plomer, Jack Sprott, and Joe Ackerley. And what survivors of Bloomsbury!—Leonard Woolf,

Duncan Grant, Clive, Vanessa and Quentin Bell, David Garnett and his wife. Then there are novelists of a younger generation, Angus Wilson, L. P. Hartley, P. H. Newby, and the familiar names from the literary weeklies, V. S. Pritchett, Raymond Mortimer, Alan Pryce-Jones, Janet Adam-Smith, Philip Toynbee, Matthew Hodgart. There are Sir William Haley and John Morris to remind us of his interest in the B.B.C., and Sir Kenneth Clark of his interest in the arts. And there is the musician Elizabeth Poston, then living at "Howards End" (Rook's Nest at Stevenage), and, of course, his great friends Bob and May Buckingham, and members of his family. On that day Morgan presented to the College a family heirloom of untold price, his first edition of William Blake's *Songs of Innocence*. It seemed somehow symbolic: he had already repaid to King's more than King's had ever been able to give; but that would not have occurred to him.

Forster and Bloomsbury

by David Garnett

"We did not see much of Forster at that time; who was already the elusive colt of a dark horse," Lord Keynes wrote[1] of the years about 1902 when he was forming his early beliefs, based on the philosophy of G. E. Moore and the discussions in the Society, otherwise known as the Apostles. Leonard Woolf lists the active Moorists as Maynard Keynes, Lytton Strachey, Saxon Sydney-Turner, Thoby Stephen and himself, "and at varying distances from the centre Clive Bell, J. T. Sheppard, R. G. Hawtrey and A. R. Ainsworth orbiting at some distance beyond". "Forster and Desmond MacCarthy," he adds, "moved erratically in and out of this solar system of intellectual friendship, like comets."[2]

The explanation of Morgan Forster's making only occasional appearances was the difference in age, which is never more important than at school or the university. He was four years older than Maynard Keynes and had gone down from Cambridge in 1901, two years before the Moorist revelation was most influential. (*Principia Ethica* was not published till 1903.) Forster would revisit Cambridge for a meeting of the Society, and, more important

[1] *Two Memoirs* (Hart-Davis, London, 1949), p. 81.
[2] *Sowing* (Hogarth Press, London, 1960), p. 171.

to him, to see Goldsworthy Lowes Dickinson, and then vanish.

Forster's friendships with Nathaniel Wedd and Dickinson were far more formative than those with any of the younger men. He must have met Moore occasionally, but he only got to know him well towards the end of Moore's life; and I have been told that Ainsworth, rather than Moore, is the model for Stewart Ansell, the young philosopher in *The Longest Journey*. Wilfred Stone has said that no one ever called Forster a Moorist, though Henry James got the two men mixed up.[3] Yet the two fundamental tenets of *Principia Ethica* underlie much of Forster's writing. By these I mean that what matter are states of mind, not necessarily associated with action, and that since it is impossible to calculate the final effects of any act one must only take into account the immediate result: thus a brutal or a barbarous action can never be justified because of its possible long-term results. Forster applies this not only to such acts as the bombing of a foreign country but to every form of unkindness.

Artists, in which term I include imaginative writers, reflect a climate of opinion rather than devote themselves to ethical propaganda; and it is the climate of opinion which Forster absorbed at Cambridge from Dickinson and his friends in the Society that one finds expressed with such subtlety in the novels.

No one has questioned that the Cambridge which produced that climate of opinion existed. But when the young men from Cambridge went to London, got married, or set up house there, did they form "Bloomsbury"? Clive Bell denied that it ever existed. But whether he was right or wrong, it has been invented, worshipped by some and abominated by others. If there was a Bloomsbury, it certainly centred round No. 46 Gordon Square, the house in which Clive Bell and Vanessa Stephen went to live after their marriage. It is arguable that the factor which distinguished the group in Cambridge after they moved to London was not a matter of space and time but the presence of two women, the daughters of Sir Leslie Stephen, Vanessa and Virginia. There

---

[3] Stone, *op. cit.* (p. 19), pp. 65–6; and E. M. Forster, "Henry James and the Young Men", *The Listener*, LXII (1959), 103.

is truth in Cyril Connolly's recent description of Bloomsbury as a "milieu which is more intense, more spacious and more loving [than our own]. Bloomsbury was such a society, matriarchal despite the brilliance of the courtiers, and at the centre of the maze sat the unwobbling pivot, Vanessa Bell."[4]

Friendships formed at the university often fall apart as life brings new experiences and interests. Work absorbs and scatters groups of friends. This did not happen to the "Bloomsburies", for several reasons. Most of them were heretics who did not accept conventional standards of art, literature, morals or ethics. They were men and women with strong intellectual interests and great originality. They were, moreover, attached to and interested in each other. These facts kept them together. And then Clive Bell was extremely hospitable.

Of the others, Virginia and her brother Adrian Stephen set up house together in Brunswick Square. Maynard Keynes, Duncan Grant and Gerald Shove took rooms in it. The whole group went to the opera, to the ballet, they gave parties and had play-readings and played poker far into the night. Naturally changes took place as the years went by. Virginia married Leonard Woolf and they had various homes, moving out to Richmond and back to Bloomsbury; Adrian Stephen married and came to live in No. 51 Gordon Square; the Strachey family left Hampstead and took No. 50 next door; James Strachey married and took No. 41 Gordon Square. Maynard Keynes married and took over the lease of No. 46. Clive took a flat at the top of Adrian's house and Vanessa took a lease of No. 37. Roger Fry went to live in Bernard Street, and Morgan Forster had a *pied-à-terre* in my mother-in-law's house, No. 27 Brunswick Square. It was of this period that Leonard Woolf writes: "It was not until Lytton Strachey, Roger Fry and Morgan Forster came into the locality, so that we were all continually meeting one another, that our society became complete."[5]

Yet Morgan Forster was on the periphery rather than at the

[4] Review of *Lytton Strachey: a Critical Biography*, vol. 2, by Michael Holroyd, in *Sunday Times Weekly Review*, 25 Feb. 1968, p. 51.
[5] *Downhill All the Way* (Hogarth Press, London, 1967), p. 114.

heart of this circle. I would not describe his visits as sudden and comet-like, blazing through the solar system. He seemed to turn up when something interesting was occurring; and he himself was always interesting. The elusiveness that Maynard Keynes notes is very characteristic, and was made more noticeable by the fact that for many years, just as the party was warming up, he had to catch a train back to Weybridge. He was more like the Cheshire Cat than a comet.

The friendship that originally brought him into Bloomsbury was that with Leonard Woolf. He had known Leonard before the latter went to Ceylon, and the friendship grew after his return. Forster had met Virginia before her marriage, but his friendship with her, based largely on their both being professional writers, only grew close because she and Leonard were a couple usually seen together. For Morgan Forster, Leonard Woolf was a practical man whose advice and help he was anxious to get in any difficulty.

When, at the beginning of 1921, he was invited to go out to India as temporary private secretary to the Maharajah of Dewas Senior, Forster thought that he ought to be able to ride a horse. He consulted Leonard and asked him to give him lessons. Leonard agreed and lessons took place at Richmond. Morgan shared the trust that so many people, particularly the young and the simple, and all animals feel for Leonard. But, if he sought Leonard's advice, Virginia came to respect and depend on his criticism and good opinion of her writing more than on that of Lytton Strachey or Clive Bell or Roger Fry. His importance to her is best described in the following passage from her diary, written after a visit by Forster to Hogarth House and a walk along the banks of the Thames:

> We talked very rarely, the proof being that we (I anyhow) did not mind silences. Morgan has the artist's mind; he says the simple things that clever people don't say; I find him the best of critics for that reason. Suddenly out comes the obvious thing that one has overlooked. He is in trouble with a novel of his own. . . .[6]

It was not a one-way traffic: Morgan's value to Virginia was

[6] *A Writer's Diary* (Hogarth Press, London, 1953), p. 21.

repaid by Leonard. After his return from India, he showed Leonard the unfinished manuscript of *A Passage to India* which he had abandoned in despair. Leonard pronounced it a great work and urged him to finish it. Moreover, his consciousness of the Bloomsbury audience consisting of his friends, Virginia and Leonard, Clive, Lytton, Maynard, and Roger had, I suspect, a restraining influence on his vein of fantasy. At the time of the early novels—1905 to 1910, when Bloomsbury was only just coming into existence—Edward Garnett had influenced him far more than the Stracheys or Stephens ever did. In these novels and in the stories Pan, satyrs and dryads sometimes make their appearance and are always present in the wings. Even in *Howards End* there are pigs' teeth in the wych-elm. Edward Garnett had told him that these sublimations or symbolisations of sex were often out of key and unconvincing, and Bloomsbury later reinforced his judgement. Morgan Forster himself recalls that "The Point of It"

> was ill-liked when it came out by my Bloomsbury friends. "What *is* the point of it?" they queried thinly, nor did I know how to reply. (css, vii.)

It is possible that without this restraining influence the immanent spirit in the Marabar caves might have become an overt presence, disastrous to the credibility of *A Passage to India*.

If Morgan Forster sought the aid of Leonard as a practical man, the situation was sometimes reversed in his relations with Lytton Strachey. In September 1915, at the end of Lytton's tenancy of Hilton Young's cottage in Wiltshire, Morgan not only helped him to pack up all his possessions, but undertook to see them safely delivered to the Strachey home in Belsize Park Gardens while Lytton went off on a round of visits. At the beginning of the friendship Morgan and Lytton had been rather shy of one another, but understanding and affection grew after the war and until Lytton's death. It was founded, not on admiration of each other's work, but on shared jokes and sympathetic appreciation of each other's attitude to life.

Another early accquaintance which grew into friendship with

the years was that with Roger Fry. Their friendship was enhanced by their interest in Charles Mauron, the French writer on aesthetics who later translated *A Passage to India*.

The first time that I met Forster in Bloomsbury was at a party given by Lady Ottoline Morrell in Bedford Square. The next day, going to Duncan Grant's studio at the top of No. 22 Fitzroy Street, I found Forster sitting there. Then the bell sounded and I ran down and admitted D. H. Lawrence and Frieda, who had also come to look at Duncan's pictures. Forster was, I think, interested to meet Lawrence again, but after one or two pictures had been set up on the easel Lawrence began a didactic harangue, and an expression of pain came into Morgan's face. I have often noticed him wince when someone has said something brutal or insensitive. Usually it is only for a moment as he braces himself to face the harshness of the outside world. But as Lawrence launched himself on a denunciation of the evil that he discovered in Duncan's paintings the look of pain was replaced by one of pure misery, and very soon he murmured something about a train to Weybridge and disappeared.

Though the wince of pain is one of my most vivid memories of Morgan Forster, the delighted appreciation of a remark which had pleased him is a more frequent memory. His broad, rather heart-shaped face would light up, the eyes would sparkle and a sort of suppressed sneeze which became a surreptitious laugh would reveal how greatly he had been pleased and amused. It was a pleasure that was almost anguish. I have most often witnessed this reaction at readings of the Memoir Club. Sometimes a preliminary look of pain would be followed by the little sneeze of joy when he listened to the inspired gossip which was characteristic of Bloomsbury—gossip which its chroniclers stigmatise as malicious, but which was actually the result of an almost gourmet-like love of the foibles of old and intimate friends. What would be malicious if told about a stranger or a slight acquaintance may be free of malice if told about a loved one. Such were the anecdotes at the expense of Vanessa and Duncan and Roger Fry. And rich and varied they were.

I myself saw most of Morgan Forster when I was a bookseller and he did more than anyone in Bloomsbury, or outside it, to help Francis Birrell and me make our shop pay its way.

He was not at that time the world-renowned author he has become. One of his introductions led to our supplying the state of Hyderabad with educational books, another to our equipping Palestine with terrestrial globes. A recommendation from him got me a job as a reviewer on the *Daily Herald* at a time when I was very hard up. After I became an author he recommended a book of mine to a Danish lady who translated it. For all these considerate and generous acts I have always been grateful. But the greatest gift was to feel that one was liked, and the greatest pleasure to watch his face light up with appreciation or approval of something one had said and to provoke the little sneeze of anguished, slightly surreptitious, laughter.

Laughter was omnipresent in Bloomsbury, but how different were its individual tones. Clive had a loud uncontrolled guffaw that did one's heart good, Virginia a sudden bird-like crow. Lytton's laughter took many forms to match the wide range of his feelings which it expressed. Leonard's and Vanessa's were often reluctant. But Morgan's appreciative, anguished, but always critical laughter is the most abiding memory I have of him among his friends in Bloomsbury.

Only Connect . . . :
Forster and India

by K. Natwar-Singh

As I write this essay affectionate recollections of Mr. Forster come rushing to my mind. I do not wish to drive them away, even though they might make a dispassionate appraisal difficult. Just as he found it impossible to resist India, his friends find it impossible to resist him. I have had the good fortune of calling Mr. Forster a friend for fifteen years; it is largely to him that I owe such awakening as has befallen me. I have said elsewhere that a part of myself, such as I am today, has been moulded and permanently influenced by him. I do not know if that would do him any credit, but without him my life would have been infinitely poorer. His writings and his personal example have made some of his readers aware, if not capable, of higher things. He cured us of some of our baser ambitions and instincts: if, to adapt a familiar saying, we can't beat them we don't want to join them either. The result is that his "aristocracy of the sensitive, the considerate and the plucky" (TC, 82) gets short shrift in the rough and tumble of everyday life. Yet it never gives up, never gives in. Its members are to be found in three generations of Indians who have had the pleasure of calling Morgan Forster a friend.

This emotional intimacy and *rapport*, spreading over most of the twentieth century, with a people so different from his own has

been achieved through affection, loyalty, a warm heart, and sensitive understanding. He has spoken with a voice unlike anybody
else's. The Indore preacher conveys much of our love for Forster
when he tells him during the Gokul Ashtami Festival: "We have
not met an Englishman like you previously." (HD, 111.)

A meeting of minds may not have always been achieved, but
the hearts did meet. The radiance of his triple vision—as friend,
critic, creative artist—has helped a few of us in "the building of
the rainbow bridge that should connect the prose in us with the
passion" so that we might "connect without bitterness until all
men are brothers" (HE, 196, 284). That is the essence of *A Passage
to India*, the reason why it endures. It is still read, not because it
found answers "to the tragic problem of India's political future"
(TC, 334), but because it promotes the creed that without love you
cannot "connect". The "undeveloped hearts" (AH, 13) which
ruled India failed to "connect": their work and labours ended in
"panic and emptiness".

In contemporary India Forster is not widely known, and judgement has been passed on him almost wholly on the basis of *A
Passage to India*. *The Hill of Devi* evoked an India that was not
popular in the 1950s; in a letter to me in 1954 Forster wrote: "Yes,
I am afraid the book will be as uncongenial to the new India as *A
Passage* was to the old Anglo-India. The outlook of both the
books is much the same. I think it is the political situation that
has altered." The later book was misunderstood as an apology for
the Princely Order. No one remembered that as long ago as 1922,
in his remarkable essay, "The Mind of the Indian Native State",
Forster had said: "An alliance between the British and the
Princes against the rest of India could only lead to universal
disaster, yet there are people on both sides who are foolish enough
to want it." (AH, 378.)

But there is a hard core of admirers who are aware of the deep
and powerful influence he had on the moral outlook of his age,
and to them he came as a blessed relief after Kipling.

Having mentioned Kipling's name, I must pause and say something about him in relation to Forster. For the first quarter of the

twentieth century the English-speaking world, perhaps including Forster, looked at India largely through the eyes of Rudyard Kipling. In his tribute to Ross Masood, Forster says—"Until I met him, India was a vague jumble of rajas, sahibs, babus and ele-phants, and I was not interested in such a jumble: who could be?" (TC, 299.) Well, a great many Englishmen were, for that is pre-cisely the India which Kipling very nearly succeeded in immortalis-ing. All that tosh about the white man's burden and the stiff upper lip which made the sahibs at Poona and Cheltenham feel so pukka only widened the gulf between India and Britain. Forster, to some extent, provided the corrective, but the damage had been done.

Sensitive Indians found Kipling's jingoism offensive and offending, and many would agree with Orwell's comment that he was "morally insensitive and aesthetically disgusting".[1] Orwell's correction of "white man's burden" to "black man's burden"[2] is is also very much to the point; for, unlike Forster, Kipling had no understanding of the economics of imperialism or for that matter any kind of economics. It was beyond him to realise or learn that the British Raj, like all other empires, was an exploitation machine. He would have been completely baffled by Martin Luther King's comment that "the peculiar genius of imperialism was found in its capacity to delude so much of the world into the belief that it was civilising primitive cultures even though it was grossly exploiting them."[3]

Forster and his like would neither build nor sustain empires; they have not the dedicated zeal, nor the self-righteous, public-school sense of responsibility upon which empires rest, as do their graves.

Forster has been to India three times. His first visit was in

[1] "Rudyard Kipling", *My Country Right or Left (Collected Essays, Journal-ism and Letters,* vol. 2; Secker & Warburg, London, and Harcourt, Brace, New York, 1968), p. 184.
[2] *ibid.,* p. 193.
[3] *The Legacy of Nehru,* ed. K. Natwar-Singh (John Day, New York, 1965), p. 67. I am indebted to the publisher for permission to quote.

1912–13, in the company of Goldsworthy Lowes Dickinson and
R. C. Trevelyan. It was during this trip that he met, through Sir
Malcolm Darling—a non-establishment Civil Servant and an
exception to the generally unattractive set of men who ruled
India—the Maharaja of Dewas Senior, Bapu Sahib, who "was
certainly a genius and possibly a saint" (HD, 49). During this
visit Forster travelled fairly extensively and made many friends.
In spite of the bomb-throwing incident at Delhi, in which the
Viceroy, Lord Hardinge, was slightly injured (HD, 18–19), the
India of 1912 was politically very dull and inactive; and the Indian
National Congress, in the words of Jawaharlal Nehru—who had
just returned to India after seven years at Harrow, Cambridge,
and London—"was very much an English-knowing upper-class
affair where morning coats and well-pressed trousers were
greatly in evidence. Essentially it was a social gathering with no
political excitement or tension."[4] Gandhi was still in South
Africa and relatively unknown.

The second visit was from April to November 1921. He spent
most of his time at Dewas, where he was private secretary to the
Maharaja. It was during this trip that Forster saw "so much
of the side of life that is hidden from most English people"
(HD, 25).

Forster's last visit to India was in 1945, when he came to attend
the Indian PEN Conference. His two great friends, Masood and
Bapu Sahib, had died in 1937. He travelled to Delhi, Calcutta,
Bombay and Hyderabad. Finally, he visited Santiniketan, "the
home and the creation of Tagore. . . . I spent a night there, and
understood why it has exercised a mystic influence on many of its
sons. You will either know a great deal about Santiniketan or else
you will never have heard of it. It is that kind of place. Its name
means 'The Home of Peace'." (TC, 334.) Tagore, of course, was
dead and so was Iqbal and "their disappearance has impoverished
the scene." (p. 333.) Forster had met them both and has written

---

[4] *An Autobiography* (Bodley Head, London, 1936), p. 27. I am grateful
to Mrs. Indira Gandhi for permission to quote this and other passages
from her father's book.

about them in *Abinger Harvest* and *Two Cheers for Democracy*. Of
this last visit he says:

> The big change I noticed was the increased interest in politics.
> You cannot understand the modern Indians unless you realise
> that politics occupy them passionately and constantly, that artistic
> problems, and even social problems—yes and even economic
> problems—are subsidiary. Their attitude is "first we must find
> the correct political solution, and then we can deal with other
> matters." I think the attitude is unsound, and used to say so;
> still, there it is, and they hold it much more vehemently than they
> did a quarter of a century ago. When I spoke about the necessity
> of form in literature and the importance of the individual vision,
> their attention wandered, although they listened politely. Litera-
> ture, in their view, should expound or inspire a political creed.
> (TC, 327–8.)

In pre-1947 India "Art for Art's Sake" was not a popular creed,
and understandably so. First the battle for independence had to
be won, then the problems of literature could be attended to.

"And did I do any good?" Forster asks himself. "Yes, I did. I
wanted to be with Indians, and was, and that is a very little step in
the right direction." (p. 335.)

Mr. Forster is perhaps the only Englishman, certainly the only
English writer, to have inspired half a dozen Indian writers to
present a book of tributes to him.

In March 1963 Santha Rama Rau and Raja Rao were in my
apartment in Manhattan. Santha's dramatisation of *A Passage to
India* was still being talked about. Raja Rao's second novel in
twenty-five years, *The Serpent and the Rope*, had received attention
in serious literary circles in America. Forster's name naturally
came up. Raja Rao said I should postpone my "study" of Forster
and edit instead an Indian tribute to him as an offering on his
eighty-fifth birthday. He added that nobody had done more for his
writing than Forster. Both his first novel *Kanthapura* and *The
Serpent and the Rope* were published with Forster's help, and became successes in their own right. So a decision was taken to get
on with the project. Forster gave his affectionate blessing and by

permitting inclusion of selections from his Indian writings—
among them his virtually unknown but deeply moving and perceptive tribute to Gandhi[5]—made publication possible.

The book, when it appeared, attracted attention in unexpected
quarters. American admirers of Forster and critics responded
warmly and it provided them an occasion to join in the *Tribute*.
It also provided an opportunity for a reappraisal of Forster's work,
its relevance and importance to present-day problems. The *Wall
Street Journal*, as befits a sound financial paper, posed the most
pertinent question:

> Few men of the West, none of them statesman, or in what C. P.
> Snow calls the corridors of power, can have had as much praise
> and of such kind from the East . . . . What was this accomplish-
> ment that won such feelings for an Englishman writing as a
> novelist about India; a circumstance that could have, and often
> has, engendered hostility?

The accomplishment is indeed of a very high order, possibly
unique. On the one hand it has been resolutely private and on the
other it has had wider, even universal, overtones. India has been a
major but by no means an exclusive influence on Forster, even
though he calls his stay in Dewas "the great opportunity of my
life" (HD, 10).

A Passage to India describes the "human predicament". It also
describes an India that has altered very considerably since 1924,
but despite subsequent works on India by Westerners, it remains
the outstanding example of an Englishman's honest effort to
understand and interpret this country and its complex people.

My theme, Forster and India, debars me from discussing the
artistic and other excellences of *A Passage to India*, and I shall con-
fine myself to its politics, which remained relevant for a very long
time. The Indian situation changed, but comparable situations
sprang up in other parts of the British Empire, and the same mistakes were made. The insolence of British administrators, the

[5] *E. M. Forster: A Tribute*, ed. K. Natwar-Singh (Harcourt, Brace, New
York, 1964), pp. 79–81.

behaviour of their wives, the thoughtless imposition of unworkable federations, continued till only the other day.

What impact, if any, did it make in England forty-five years
ago? What impact did it make in India? Forster has himself provided an answer to the first question. In 1962 I asked him what
were the Indian and British reactions to *A Passage to India* when it
appeared in 1924.

> EMF: For a long time no one took any notice. Then a paper called
> the *Morning Post* reviewed it favourably. After a year or two it
> started—the reactions to the book, I mean. I also received a few
> abusive letters from Anglo-Indians.
>
> Q: What is your own assessment of the political influence it had
> on the "Indian question" of the time? Do you think its political
> influence was accidental and exaggerated?
>
> EMF: It had some political influence—it caused people to think
> of the link between India and Britain and to doubt if that link
> was altogether of a healthy nature. The influence (political) was
> not intended; I was interested in the story and the characters. But
> I welcomed it.[6]

There is no doubt that thoughtful, honest, liberal-minded
Englishmen and intellectuals both in the Government and outside
began to look at the Indian situation from a different point of
view.

The literary intelligentsia were shocked and deeply disturbed.
Forster made the British Raj stick in their throats, and it wasn't a
comfortable or comforting sensation to live with. Looking beyond and beneath the brilliance of the writing, they began to ask:
"What are we up to in India?" As a novelist it was not Forster's
responsibility to find political solutions. Morally there could be
no justification for one race ruling over another. The problem was
posed and an indictment made: the British Raj might win a few
battles, but it was losing the war. The English and the Indians
could not be friends as long as the Raj lasted. That Indo-British
relations took the turn they did during Mountbatten's time is a

[6] *ibid.*, pp. xii–xiii.

vindication of what Aziz says to Fielding at the end of the book. Hope was not abandoned; it was only postponed.

Forster was the first English writer to portray Indians as human beings and not merely as caricatures or doubtful and shifty natives. But he is no Indophile. There are indignant and highly critical portions in *Passage* and in *Devi*. He noticed and commented on our inattention to detail, our idleness and incompetence. The Hindu's preoccupation with intrigue and suspicion did not go unnoticed. "Intelligent though they are over intrigues, Indians too can get confused and identify hopes with facts. One is reduced—as are they—to siding with the people one likes. . . ." (HD, 66.) He was helpless in the presence of the widespread Hindu habit of referring to almost all religious and metaphysical matters by a periphrasis.

We took it from him (even Godbole's highbrow incoherence) for two reasons. First, because he was harder on his own people, whose reaction, indeed, proved that "nothing enrages Anglo-India more than the lantern of reason if it is exhibited for one moment after its extinction is decreed." (PI, 173.) Second, because he seems to have taken to heart the words of Tagore: "Come inside India, accept all her good and evil: if there be deformity then try and cure it from within, but see it with your own eyes, understand it, think over it, turn your face towards it, become one with it."[7]

Forster's portrayal of Anglo-India has been disapprovingly commented upon. It has been labelled as exaggerated and uncharitable. But this view does not stand up to close scrutiny. The men who "ruled India" *did* behave badly, *did* snub Indians, while their women "knew none of the politer forms [of Urdu] and of the verbs only the imperative mood" (PI, 45). They constantly outraged Indian sentiments. Even after independence sections of the British community in certain cities ran their own clubs on racial lines. Such behaviour was not likely to endear them to a free India

[7] These words from Rabindranath Tagore's novel, *Gora* (Macmillan, London, 1924), pp. 102–3, are quoted on the title-page of Sir Malcolm Darling's *Rusticus Loquitur* (Oxford University Press, London, 1930).

any more than that of their fathers had endeared them to Forster.

Does Forster do injustice to the British Civil Servants in India?
Is he unfair to them? Let us call Nehru as witness:

> They lived in a narrow, circumscribed world of their own—
> Anglo-India—which was neither England nor India. They had
> no appreciation of the forces at work in contemporary society. In
> spite of their amusing assumption of being the trustees and
> guardians of the Indian masses, they knew little about them and
> even less about the new aggressive bourgeoisie. They judged
> Indians from the sycophants and office-seekers who surrounded
> them and dismissed others as agitators and knaves. Their know-
> ledge of post-war changes all over the world, and especially in
> the economic sphere, was of the slightest, and they were too
> much in the ruts to adjust themselves to changing conditions.
> They did not realise that the order they represented was out of
> date under modern conditions, and that they were approaching
> as a group more and more the type which T. S. Eliot describes
> in "The Hollow Men".[8]

Forster would have been spared a great deal of criticism if more
people in India had read Rose Macaulay's comment: "Some confusion is perhaps caused by the book's doubtful chronology, for it
deals with the India of one period, is written largely from material
collected and from a point of view derived from that period, and
was published twelve years later, when Indians and English had
got into quite another stage."[9] The "doubtful chronology" of the
book did indeed create confusion. It depicts a pre-1914 India and
by the time it was published in 1924 events had overtaken it. It
appears to be an almost anti-nationalist book, since it makes no
mention of the political ferment that was going on in India in the
early 'twenties.

The First World War had changed everything. The Montagu-
Chelmsford reforms had not fully met Indian aspirations, Gandhi
had launched his non-cooperation movement, Tagore had re-
nounced his knighthood after General Dyer had killed 379 peaceful

[8] Nehru, *op. cit.*, p. 443.
[9] *The Writings of E. M. Forster* (Hogarth Press, London, 1938), p. 188.

Indians in cold blood in Jallianwallah Bagh. After this, Gandhi, who till then had tolerated the British Raj, became its most outspoken opponent. The book therefore, failed to impress the Indian nationalists, who consisted largely of middle-class intellectuals. It made little or no impact in India. The issues had gone beyond good manners. It succeeded in annoying the British without satisfying Indian political aspirations. Gandhi did not read it, and the highly intelligent and erudite C. Rajagopalachari, the man who succeeded Mountbatten as the first and last Indian Governor-General, did not do so till quite recently. Nehru did, and refers to it in his *Autobiography*.

It seems odd that a person of Forster's awareness could have been so totally oblivious of what was going on in India in 1921. It is typical of him not to have explained, or to have tried to explain it away. We had to wait for *The Hill of Devi* to solve the mystery, and even that only on a very close reading.

In a recent article in *Encounter* Andrew Shonfield says that "Forster had little understanding and no sympathy for the complicated and courageous politics of the Indian independence movement."[10] Forster's political antennae were a little more acute and active than Mr. Shonfield imagines. Writing about the visit of the Prince of Wales in 1921, Forster in places sounds amazingly like Nehru—although this was the year which saw Nehru in prison for the first time.

> About the Prince of Wales's visit I might also write much. It is disliked and dreaded by nearly everyone. The chief exceptions are the motor-firms and caterers, who will make fortunes, and the non-cooperators and extremists, who will have an opportunity for protest which they would otherwise have lacked. . . . The National Congress meets in December at Ahmedabad, and it will certainly carry through its resolution in favour of Civil Disobedience, and if there is general response, this expensive royal expedition will look rather foolish. I have been with pro-Govt and pro-English Indians all this time, so cannot realise the feeling of the other party; and am only sure of this—that we are paying for the insolence of Englishmen *and* Englishwomen out herin

[10] *Encounter,* XXX (Jan. 1968), 68.

the past. I don't mean that good manners can avert a political upheaval. But they can minimise it, and come nearer to averting it in the East than elsewhere. . . . But it's too late. Indians don't long for social intercourse with Englishmen any longer. They have made a life of their own. (HD, 154–5.)

Nehru says much the same thing in his *Autobiography* which *The Hill of Devi* preceded by nearly fifteen years.

G. Lowes Dickinson is reported by E. M. Forster, in his recent life of him, to have once said about India: "And *why* can't the races meet? Simply because the Indians *bore* the English. *That* is the simple adamantine fact." It is possible that most English-men feel that way and it is not surprising. To quote Forster again (from another book), every Englishman in India feels and behaves, and rightly, as if he was a member of an army of occu-pation, and it is quite impossible for natural and unrestrained rela-tions between the two races to grow under these circumstances. The Englishman and the Indian are always posing to each other and naturally they feel uncomfortable in each other's company. Each bores the other and is glad to get away from him to breathe freely and move naturally again.

Usually the Englishman meets the same set of Indians, those connected with the official world, and he seldom reaches really interesting people, and if he reached them he would not easily draw them out. The British regime in India has pushed up into prominence, even socially, the official class, both British and Indian, and this class is most singularly dull and narrow-minded. Even a bright young Englishman on coming out to India will soon relapse into a kind of intellectual and cultural torpor and will get cut off from all live ideas and movements. After a day in office, dealing with the ever-rotating and never-ending files, he will have some exercise and then go to his club to mix with his kind, drink whisky and read *Punch* and the illustrated weeklies from England. He hardly reads books and if he does he will probably go back to an old favourite. And for this gradual deterioration of mind he will blame India, curse the climate, and generally anathematise the tribe of agitators who add to his troubles, not realising that the cause of intellectual and cultural decay lies in the hide-bound bureaucratic and despotic system of govern-ment which flourishes in India and of which he is a tiny part.[11]

[11] Nehru, *op. cit.*, pp. 28–9.

Forster always warmed to talk about Jawaharlal Nehru. He met Nehru twice and recalled these meetings with feeling. Nehru's style, his secularism, his internationalism, his quiet but open agnosticism, all appealed to Forster and he was, even when not wholly approving of the turn the Indian National movement was taking, horrified that men like Gandhi and Nehru should be denied the freedom to say their say. Forster once said to me: "Nehru is the most upright and level-headed statesman in the world. Politicians are generally busy tidying up their past. Your Prime Minister is an exception." In 1964, a few weeks after Nehru's death, I gave Forster a copy of Nehru's last will and testament. Forster was visibly moved and said how saddened he was at Nehru's passing away. He told an American friend of mine that he "would have voted for Nehru with both hands."[12]

Forster has also been taken to task for choosing a Moslem as the main character in his novel. This hasn't worried the Indians too much. Even after partition sixty million co-religionists of Aziz live in India. Islam is their religion, India their home. That Aziz had been taken as *the* Moslem and Godbole as *the* Hindu is unfortunate. It is wrong and dangerous to talk in such confined terms. Just as there is no such thing as the real India, there is no single individual representing an entire community. Forster as a novelist and creative artist was free to choose anyone for his hero. His choice does not make him pro-Moslem or anti-Hindu. The community of the person was unimportant for describing and high-lighting the human predicament, and for describing human relationships.

Forster himself told me: "I think of them—of Aziz and Godbole—as people and not as religious types." And I am content to leave it at that. Forster has many Moslem friends, and a larger number of Hindu friends. It is a matter of chance and not of calculation.

The Hill of Devi finally nails the lie that Forster does not know his Hindu well. Even given Forster's insight into human character,

[12] In July 1964 I visited Forster, accompanied by an American friend, Jane Goldstone (now Mrs. Ralph Feaver). She kept a record of the meeting and I quote this with her permission.

his gift for finding the right words for the right occasions, his talent for uncovering layer after layer of the human personality, his sturdy moral realism, his aesthetic sense and his sense of the unseen, no one who had not made a study of Hindu philosophy and thought could have written such a book. Raja Rao calls it "one of the most Indian books of this century".[13] Whether he writes about Hindus or Moslems, he penetrates their hearts and the result is dazzling. The sheer authenticity of the dialogue in both books is staggering. His description of the Gokul Ashtami festival is flawless. Forster caught the *spirit* of the festival and found meaning and significance in Hindu ritual which have eluded or escaped other English writers.

He also took the trouble to study the Bhagavad-Gita. Without such a study, his description of Gokul Ashtami would have been superficial. A Hindu festival made him aware of a gap in Christianity: "the canonical gospels do not record that Christ laughed or played. Can a man be perfect if he never laughs or plays? Krishna's jokes may be vapid, but they bridge a gap." (HD, 119.)

Forster had obviously read the Bhagavad-Gita either before or during his first visit in 1912. His essay "Hymn before Action" deserves to be better known. It analyses the central core of the Gita. Krishna asks Arjuna to fight and destroy his enemies even though they be his close relatives. Arjuna must fight because it is his duty and that duty has not been assigned to him by chance. Krishna convinces Arjuna, who drives into battle rejoicing, and wins a great victory. "But it is necessarily and rightly followed by disillusionment and remorse. The fall of his enemies leads to his own, for the fortunes of men are all bound up together, and it is impossible to inflict damage without receiving it." (AH, 382.)

Forster has acknowledged his debt to India and Indians. It is time we acknowledged our debt to him. Even at the best of times Forster has been aware of the excesses of nationalism and for a long time his attitude to Indian nationalism was cautiously sympathetic, not noisy and erratic like Bertrand Russell's. In spite of hating "causes", he has consistently, quietly, and candidly stood up

[13] *E. M. Forster: A Tribute*, p. 28.

for India. When many of the professional and loud-mouthed
British friends of India looked the other way, he came out strongly
in support of India at the time of the Chinese aggression in 1962.

> We can urge on our Government and the Governments of the
> West to supply arms on lend lease, and to increase the aid they
> give for India's Plans, now that India's own resources have so
> largely to be devoted to war. Above all, we must try to give
> additional heart and courage to our Indian friends whose spirit
> in the crisis is sound and steadfast. On the survival and success of
> India depends the hope for a better life of one-fifth of the human
> race. We cannot let the Chinese aggressors destroy this hope.[14]

During the Second World War, as President of the National
Council for Civil Liberties, he took up the cudgels on behalf of
Jaya Prakash Narayan, who was being tortured in Lahore jail. He
was appalled that his countrymen should treat brave patriots like
Jaya Prakash Narayan in this brutal manner.

Since personal relationships are at the centre of Forster's creed,
it is appropriate to end on a personal note. Without his support
and backing the careers of some of India's leading writers would
not have been possible. I have already mentioned Raja Rao and
Santha Rama Rau. Mulk Raj Anand told me that in 1935 Forster
saved him from suicide by adding a preface to his first novel *Un-
touchable*, which had been rejected by seventeen publishers. His
generous intervention in 1940 for Ahmed Ali's novel *Twilight in
Delhi*, his discriminating observations about R. K. Narayan, G. V.
Desani, and Narayan Menon illustrate his belief that the Indian
talent is no less significant than any other, given the chance. His
has been truly "the face of a friend" (AH, 337) and what he said of
Gandhi is in no small measure applicable to himself:

> He is with all the men and women who have sought something
> in life that is neither chaos nor mechanism, who have not con-
> fused happiness with possessiveness, or victory with success, and
> who have believed in love.[15]

[14] Letter by E. M. Forster and others in *The Spectator*, CCIX (30 Nov.
1962), p. 856.
[15] *E. M. Forster: A Tribute*, p. 81.

Forster in Rumania

by Alec Randall

E M. Forster became friends with my wife and me, and with
our small children, when we went to live in Weybridge. This
was in 1924, the year of his first best-selling novel, *A Passage to
India*, of which he gave me a copy. I think it was through our
children that we first came to know Morgan and his mother, who
had a house in Weybridge. Those children who were old enough
went to a school for small children kept by a Miss Gilpin, near
our house. She was related to Michael Sadleir, whose children
went to the same school, and Morgan was a friend of Miss Gilpin's. She was a genius in educating, stimulating, and encouraging
spontaneity in young children; and her school was a happy little
community. Morgan admired Miss Gilpin,[1] and we came to share
his admiration; we felt grateful for the way she and her staff introduced our two small daughters to music and poetry, sums and
history. They treasured a French nativity play which the school
did at Christmas, and which, with some friends, they later acted in
our house in Bucharest. I must add that we became equally good
friends with Morgan's mother, shrewd, witty, lovable; she treated

[1] He had twice reviewed plays performed by her pupils—once in *The
Athenaeum* (25 July 1919) and once in the *Manchester Guardian* (8
December 1920).

small children so naturally and persuasively that they came to enjoy their visits to her, which were kept up after both Forsters had moved to Abinger Hammer.

Remembering Morgan's admirable understanding of Italy and the Italians as shown in *A Room with a View* and *Where Angels Fear to Tread*, we asked him to come and see us when, in 1926, we were settled in Rome, where I was a secretary to the British Legation to the Holy See. His reply to the invitation—"I don't want to visit a country where Cecily is not allowed to say what she thinks of the bread"—requires some explanation. In the summer my wife went with the four children to a small resort on the Tuscan coast, Castiglioncello. I used to join them at week-ends, and one day my wife told me that Cecily had caused something of a scandal. Mussolini had decreed, as part of an economy campaign, that a standard loaf should be imposed on the country. When given a slice of this at breakfast Cecily protested loudly. Her Italian nurse told her that that kind man Mussolini had had the bread made especially. Cecily's only reply, in Italian, was that "Mussolini is a bad man to make us eat this nasty bread." The proprietor of the hotel came over to my wife in a state of alarm, and begged her to restrain her daughter; the child's remarks, he said, would be reported to the local *Fascio* and this could possibly mean the closing of his hotel. Morgan kept his word: he did not set foot in Italy until, so far as I remember, some time in the early 'fifties; I saw him at the club we both belonged to, the Reform, just before he took the plane to Rome.

Soon after Easter 1931 the Foreign Office transferred me to Bucharest, to be First Secretary of the British Legation there. When I had found a suitable home for the whole family we invited Morgan to come and see us. Bucharest, of course, had made a disagreeable first impression in comparison with Rome, but as we got to know it better, and explored the beautiful countryside, in spite of the atrocious roads, we liked Rumania more and more. Those were happy years. Morgan accepted the invitation. We were delighted, as were the children, who remembered "Uncle Morgan", and it was arranged that I should take the weekly diplomatic bag to

Budapest (where the King's Messenger travelling from Istanbul collected it and took it on to London), and there meet Morgan.

We met in Budapest on 28 May 1932. Both that day and the next, which was a Sunday, we saw the sights of the Hungarian capital, the beautiful upper city of Buda, the delightful Margrit Island in the Danube, the fine gallery of paintings. But on Sunday we met with a passionate display of Hungarian nationalism which rather shook us. There was a big procession, with scores of brightly coloured banners, and rabble-rousing orators. We could not understand their shouting, but were told its gist, which was that never would the Hungarian people submit to the loss of their lands to the Rumanians. The lands in question were Transylvania, which, after the First World War, Hungary had been obliged to yield to Rumania. This operation did justice to the four million or so Rumanians who had lived under Hungarian rule in the Habsburg Empire, but also transferred some two million Hungarians to Rumanian rule. We at the Legation were familiar with the situation of this large minority, since their grievances were continually sent to the League of Nations under the Minorities Treaty, and had to be looked into and reported on to the Foreign Office. But Morgan's gentle, rational mind was deeply disturbed by this display of perfervid nationalism, of which we had another sample before we left Budapest. I had to return to Bucharest direct, but Morgan wanted to see something of Transylvania on his way to Bucharest, and I introduced him to the British Consul at Cluj, as the Rumanians called this important city of Transsylvania. When I handed in a telegram to the Consul, the clerk refused to accept it. He pointed to the offending word, and only agreed to send the telegram when I had substituted Koloszvar, the Hungarian name.

My wife and I met Morgan at six in the morning of 3 June, at the Bucharest main station. He had visited also Sibiu, a predominantly German town, attractive, with interesting churches and a museum. Later that same day he came with us to the party the Minister and his wife, Sir Michael and Lady Palairet, gave for the King's birthday. Morgan was delighted to hear music from

Dinicu's gypsy band which we of the Legation, and, in fact, everyone who liked music, knew very well. Grigoraș Dinicu was a
staunch gypsy. We knew him personally and always had a chat
and a drink with him when we went to the restaurant in which he
played. He was a very fine violinist and could, we were con-
vinced, have made a career as a classical violin-player. But, as he
one day told me, he and his band supported so many of his relations that he couldn't take the risk. This family solidarity is
typical of gypsies. One of Dinicu's famous virtuoso pieces, *Cio-
carlia* ('The Lark), in which he imitated the rise of the lark in the
air and its gradual descent, was, I believe, adopted by Heifetz as
an encore. Violinists of that eminence usually went to see Dinicu
when they visited Bucharest.

Morgan's visit was not an official one. His reticent nature and
modesty kept him as a rule from public appearances and perfunc-
tory oratory, even in connection with causes he had very much at
heart. (He was a masterly broadcaster, and his writing on behalf
of organisations he supported was earnest and effective in a quiet,
persuasive way.) All the same I informed the Rumanian Foreign
Office and the PEN Club that this distinguished English writer
was visiting their country, and they responded, as I think will be
seen, in ways that Morgan found agreeable. For most of the time
he went on excursions with us, and often the children were happy
to be in the party with "Uncle Morgan". He met many of our
friends, Rumanian and Russian—the latter including the Nabokov
family, who had been driven into exile by the Bolshevik Revolution, and eventually joined the large Russian colony in Bucharest.
The father had been governor of Courland, and held some position at the Tsar's court, where his fine bass voice was often called
upon. In his old age he still sang very well. He earned the family
living by working as a cashier in a tobacco shop, and I never heard
from him any complaint about his lot, and never a word against
the Bolsheviks. He and his wife were deeply religious Orthodox.

We took Morgan to our cottage in the sub-Carpathians, near
Predeal, formerly on the border with Hungary. It was a delightful
spot at almost all times of the year, and we showed Morgan the

charming town of Brașov, where we did our marketing, during
which we could hear German, Rumanian, and Hungarian.

One of our excursions might have had very unpleasant consequences. A big attraction of Rumania in those days was the spontaneous and natural pleasure the peasants, more than ninety per
cent of the population, took in their traditional costumes and
dances. They did not perform for the benefit of tourists. On fine
Sundays, on a piece of waste land near our house, there was
dancing, and in fine weather you could hardly travel round the
countryside without meeting in villages a large group of dancers,
with a fiddler in the middle of the circle, the women dressed in
their brightly coloured skirts and embroidered blouses, the men
in breeches, embroidered jackets, and blouses hanging down
below their jackets. The designs were traditional for each region;
some sober, others gay, all in good taste. Traditional dress was
worn on working days, too, but for festive occasions the em-
broidery and so on was much more elaborate. Morgan had
admired the women's aprons we saw during one of our Sunday
excursions; they were richly embroidered and studded with silver
sequins. He wanted to buy one to give to his mother. So my wife
found the best place for getting such aprons, and the fair price to
pay. It was in Transylvania, and we decided to combine the buy-
ing with a picnic in the hills; the weather was fine but very warm.
On the way we proposed to show Morgan the castle of Bran, residence of the King's mother, the well-known Queen Marie of
Rumania. The bargaining over the aprons took a long time, but
at last Morgan and I, with all four children, got into our car,
and my wife drove off. We made our way to the hills; we were
hungry and eager for our lunch out of doors.

As we entered a village, however, my wife, driving very
slowly, sounded the horn to warn a peasant who was walking
beside a horse and cart. Instead of moving out of the way he
stepped right in front of the car, and was knocked over. Morgan
and I got out to see whether he was injured. He had picked himself up, and was obviously not hurt; he eagerly accepted the glass
of wine we offered him. We got back into the car, only to find that

our way was barred by a group of screaming women, who said
that we had injured their brother (father, cousin, uncle, etc.) and
must pay compensation. They had caught sight of the embroidered
aprons in the car, and assumed we were rich foreigners, so they
demanded 10,000 lei, about £12. I had nothing like that sum on
me, and in any case I realised that if I paid I should be open to
blackmail, and should get nothing from my insurance company.
One of our friends had been held up in the same way through
running over a pig which the peasants had driven in front of his
car; he stayed firm, and got away after making a small payment;
the pig, anyway, wasn't injured. I said that I would pay if a "pro-
tocol" was drawn up, that is, a description of the accident and an
assessment of the compensation to be paid. They fiercely refused,
and I noticed that the women had been joined by some men, who
held stones in their hands behind their backs. Obviously it
would have been dangerous for my wife to drive on; so we told
the children to crouch down away from the windows, and settled
down to wait. The old man had completely recovered and joined
the crowd, but was not abusive.

I recalled that Rumanians showed great respect for the gendarmerie, and asked Morgan if he thought it would be all right
for me to walk back some half a mile to the nearest gendarmerie
post. He and my wife agreed. The young gendarme in charge
said that his superior would come to the place I indicated as soon
as he returned. I walked back, and my wife told me that the old
man had come round and quietly offered to settle for 100 lei, about
half a crown. The problem then was to escape from the angry
relations, who all expected to get far more. Morgan said: "Tell
me the Rumanian for 100 lei." So I told him: "O suta de lei." He
then stood on the running-board, waved the note and called out
"O suta de lei . . ." while my wife gradually turned the car
round. Finally he threw the note to the crowd, who swooped on
it, and so my wife was able to get the car started in the direction
from which we had come. In a few minutes we came up with the
puffing, sweating gendarme. I told him the trouble was over, but
he insisted on going back to inspect and make a report. Soon we

caught up with the old man and his relations, and when he saw us the old man put on an exaggerated limp, and groaned. The gendarme made him come back to the spot where he had been knocked down, and take down his trousers—the women modestly looking away. "There isn't any injury," the gendarme said; "have you given him any money?" "Only 100 lei," I said. "Give it back," the gendarme shouted to the old man, who at that ran away. The gendarme would accept only a small packet of cigarettes as a tip. At that time, no doubt still (and also in other countries) gendarmes for a particular region were chosen from an entirely different region, to avoid local favouritism. So it was on this occasion. As we drove the gendarme back to his post he told us he came from the Dobrudja, and said, "Those Transylvanians are bad people," adding that the old man was a well-known character in the village and had walked with a limp for years.

Morgan came for several other excursions with us, but none so exciting as this hold-up. With Rumanian friends we went to see the fine Byzantine churches at Curtea de Argesh, and then up the wooded hill in a forestry-train, fuelled by wood, and likely, so it seemed to me, to slide back as it laboured up the steep incline. At the top, looking down on the lovely valley, our hosts had got ready for us an excellent lunch, trout straight from the mountain stream, and sheeps' milk cheese, packed in pine-bark. Morgan and all of us found this delicious. We went down in an open truck, travelling by its own momentum, and without any brakes, so far as I could see. The Rumanians said accidents were very rare, though now and then a cow or a pig would get in the way, and of the two a pig was far more dangerous. As we took our places I noticed Rumanian peasants energetically crossing themselves when a priest got into the truck. Here, and I had experienced the same thing in southern Italy, there was a superstition that priests bring bad luck.

Morgan was the guest of honour at a dinner given by the Rumanian PEN Club. It was a very pleasant occasion, but there were no fluent speakers of English, and I doubted whether any of the Rumanians present had ever read anything by him. English language and literature were at this time much neglected in Bucharest. There was no Chair of English at the University, and when we pointed out that there were Chairs of French, Italian, and German we were told that they were maintained by the governments concerned. There was a keen Anglo-Rumanian Society, but no British Council to assist in making our language and culture generally better known to foreigners. I believe that the representations the Legation made at this time on this question played some part in the decision to establish the British Council. The President of PEN, who was very amiable, though his English was rudimentary, explained that he was a passionate angler, and had picked up his English from Hardy's catalogues—the well-known London supplier of fishing-tackle. His second language, as with all educated Rumanians, was French.

Another occasion on which we accompanied Morgan was an invitation to a small picturesque town not very far from Bucharest. At our reception by the various officials or civic dignitaries on whom we called we took the traditional cup of Turkish coffee and a spoonful of rose-petal jam. Before the lunch we were also plied with pieces of fat fried bacon, with which we had glasses of *ţuica* (plum-brandy). After this, and a substantial lunch in a hall which was excessively hot, we found the organisers had been thoughtful enough to provide us with beds in various private houses, where we could take a regular siesta. Refreshed by sleep, we got up and saw some charming displays of traditional Rumanian dancing, with folk-songs. As we left the *Marseillaise* was played, for some reason I never discovered. An unusual item in the programme the officials had arranged for Morgan was a visit to a prison. I had told them he was an enthusiastic supporter of the Howard League for Penal Reform, so we were both received courteously by the governor of the Doftana prison, and shown round what I judged to be rather a show-place. Most of the prisoners were at work doing carpentry, or weaving; the governor told us that they were allowed to sell their work. Food and hygiene seemed to be adequate. But the solitary confinement cells were grim. In one of them a man in early middle age, behind bars like a cage in the

London Zoo, lay on the bare stone floor, unkempt, giving no sign of life. We were told he had been a notorious Communist rebel, condemned to a life sentence for murdering several people. The sight depressed us both.

Besides the PEN Club several other people entertained Morgan: the British Minister and Lady Palairet, and some neighbours of ours, Prince and Princess Brancoveanu, whose children were about the same age as ours, and played with them in their lovely garden. They were leading members of the small class of Rumanian landed aristocracy—small, that is, after the big break-up of large estates and assignment of land to the peasants that came after the First World War. The Brancoveanus were of the French tradition, the Princess's mother being a French marquise; and they had a paternalist attitude to the country's social problems. They maintained a hospital entirely at their own expense, filling a serious gap since the church estates, on whose revenues several hospitals were kept up, had been confiscated. The State had by no means made up this loss. At dinner the family's French tutor—for the three young sons—sat neglected at the foot of the table, and I thought it characteristic of Morgan that he should, when dinner was over, single out this young man, and have a long talk with him, rather than with some of the exalted guests. I recalled this episode when, many years later, after the Second World War, I listened to Morgan's delightful broadcast about his experiences as a tutor, fresh from Cambridge, to the children of the Countess von Arnim, author of *Elizabeth and her German Garden*. He told how two world wars had not broken the friendship he then formed with the young German tutor, who later became a Lutheran pastor.

Morgan left us on 17 June for Cracow. A few days later he published in *The Spectator* (25 June 1932) an article about the fair-haired children whom the Pied Piper of Hamelin led through the mountains from Germany to Rumania—a legend to explain the large and compact German settlements in Rumania. I once asked Morgan why he had written nothing else about his experiences in Rumania, and he said that he had, in letters to his mother. These have not been published, so I have tried to fill the gap, and give some account of the delightful and at times adventurous interlude, when Morgan gave so much pleasure to my wife and myself, to our children, and to so many excellent friends of ours in those far-off but still well-remembered days.

Forster and America

by William Roerick

Although it was Christopher Isherwood who introduced me to E. M. Forster, I must confess immediately that I am not a camera. We met in 1943 when I was a corporal in the United States Army and stationed, for a time, in England. He showed me great kindness. He has continued to do so for a quarter of a century and I am grateful, but when it comes to public accounting I find it difficult to be a public accountant. I kept no diary and made few and imprecise mental notes. I am a faulty memorist. But then it is not Forster whom I know; it is someone called Morgan.

Morgan was sixty-eight when Harvard University invited him to come to America and give an address on "The *Raison d'Etre* of Criticism in the Arts". He refused. I should say he intended to refuse. He wrote to me (I have no connection with Harvard), giving his reasons for not coming and a regret. The regret was that he would not be seeing his friends; the reasons: he was not sure that he had anything pertinent to say to a symposium of musicologists and he was not sure at sixty-eight that he could take on a new country.

America does persist in being the New World, despite centuries of habitation by people from the old and despite signs, disturbing to those of us who love it, that it may have a built-in obsolescence. Still, we are primarily the chromium-steel-concrete-rush-rush-rush country. Our occasional Whitman or Thoreau or Melville is not strong enough to affect the impression which we make on most of the world, nor even strong enough to affect most Americans. There is, however, another America in which slow or quick kindnesses do occur between individuals, in which places have survived, despite planners and despoilers. This is the America which I knew would please Morgan.

I rapidly wrote a three-page letter urging him to come over. Then I copied it out in the hope of legibility and sent it off. It brushed aside his claims of age and inadjustability. It pointed out that anything he might choose to say on any subject was certain to be of interest to a great many. I do not believe this argument swayed him. One tends not to listen attentively to compliments, even when they are accurate. What did sway him in our direction was the suggestion that he come a month early, visit his friends here and adjust slowly to the place. He accepted Harvard's invitation. He came a month early, in April of 1947.

When we spotted each other at La Guardia airport he smiled and adjusted his tweed cap. It did not need adjusting. His friends will recognise the gesture. He makes it as a joke. Perhaps I might say something about Morgan's looks. He is almost unphotographable. His looks depend on what he is thinking and feeling and saying at the moment and to whom. When a camera approaches he looks at it, it looks at him, and they have nothing to say to each other. He produces an official silence, the camera produces an unlikeness. When caught unaware in a snapshot he sometimes looks quite like himself.

We drove toward Manhattan. He saw for the first time the handsome vertical skyline of the city. He must have said something. But what?

As we passed a grocery shop on Third Avenue he exclaimed over the beautiful rows of oranges sitting precisely in the sun. Italy! Such masses of fresh fruit. He hadn't seen their like in years. I remembered, sadly, how gastronomically drab life was for

England. That courageous and admirable nation had lost who-knows-what of comfort and large or small luxury. I now remember, and rather irrelevantly include, Morgan saying of wartime cooking: "I think the English have taken the war as an excuse to indulge the innate squalor of their palate."

My mother was then living in New York at 91 Marble Hill Avenue, on the top two floors of a converted house. Housing being short after the war, she housed my sister, brother-in-law, my friend Tom Coley, and me. A shift of occupants on to cots and into the attic made it possible for her to house Morgan. He would have been troubled had he been aware of the shift when he arrived. He never wants to cause bother. Luckily, by the time he learned of the arrangement the household had showed itself to be so casual that the cots in the attic were accepted as two more bits of nonsense.

The easiest approach to the apartment was up the back stairs and through the kitchen. Morgan was given a key and that is how he came and went.

The first evening we all gathered for cocktails before dinner. My brother-in-law's speciality is the Manhattan, a drink made of a good deal of rye whisky and a hint of Italian vermouth. We had Manhattans. By the time we sat down to dinner the conversation was loud and overlapping and plentifully interspersed with laughter. Something ridiculous was said. We all laughed. Tom leaned back in his chair. There was a splintering of wood. Tom's lean continued, he disappeared completely from the table, his chair crashing under him. He was not hurt. His chair was. It was Victorian and never had been strong. The laughter continued. So, for much too long, did the barking of my sister's spoiled Dachshund, "Minky", who had concealed himself under the table in the hope that something to his liking would fall to the floor. He was not prepared for or pleased with what fell.

The story is not much of a one. It is meant, merely, to show the sort of America in which Morgan found himself.

Morgan presented one problem to my mother. She could not figure how to make up his bed properly. One half of it, from head to foot, was occupied by books, letters, reading-glasses, and oranges. She compromised her standards and remade only the edge he slept on, fearing there might be some secret system to this apparent disorder.

While in New York Morgan got to the theatre a bit. He admired Menotti's *The Medium* and *The Telephone* and told him so. He did not admire the melodrama Tom Coley was appearing in and told him so. "I was delighted to see you, dear Tom, but it is a ratty little play, isn't it?" It was indeed. He saw Ethel Merman in *Annie Get Your Gun*. At first the very Americanness of the sound made difficulties. Morgan heard Merman, but couldn't quite believe what he was hearing. Ultimately he was enchanted. In the finale of the first act, Annie is made a member of the Sioux tribe. She sings "I'm an Indian too . . . a Sioux." She tries ineptly to imitate the gestures and dances of her new tribe. The earnest effort and obvious failure were beautifully comedic. In the interval Morgan, still chuckling, said: "But she was so civil to the Indians!"

Part of the plan for easing Morgan into America was that he spend some time in Tyringham, a quiet valley in western Massachusetts, just over a hundred miles north of New York, in a region which we call the Berkshires. My own house, Lost Farm, is uninhabitable in cold weather. Even in midsummer it is considered so by many. My kind neighbours, the John Rudds, lent us their comfortable and centrally heated house.

We arrived at night, built a good three-log fire and toasted ourselves as Morgan read me the address which he had written for the Harvard symposium. When he finished he asked: "What do you think of it?" "It has marvellous stuff in it, but has it a form?" "It hasn't!" He laughed. "But that is your fault. You got me to come at the last minute and all I could do was put down whatever came into my head. It's too late now to give it a shape." (He said something like that. The ideas are correct and the good humour, if not the precise words.)

I thought, as he was reading, that I could see a possible shape. I asked if he had a carbon copy. He had. Might it be cut up and pasted together in a different order? It might. I took up the scissors as Morgan started for bed. He stopped in the doorway. "Just be sure that it says 'Love' at the beginning, in the middle and at the end."

I'm not at all certain that I really improved the address. I did collect related material into bundles. I did shift the order of attack and defence and I did salvage two jokes which Morgan had bracketed as being too flippant to come near the close. They ended up in a more central position.

The next morning Morgan read the suggested revisions. He sat down at the dining-room table and set to work. The clipping and juxtaposing had taken sections which had once followed and placed them before their antecedents. Morgan looked up and said: "You have put the spade into the soil and turned it over. It had to be turned over, but you cut through all those worms, which must now be sewn together or destroyed." And he went back to his healing and destroying.

I strike you as having been impertinent? Perhaps I was, but Morgan invites honesty and, unlike many who do so, welcomes it.

Morgan had his own travel plans. They included the Grand Canyon of the Colorado and Hamilton College, in upper New York State. That small college community was astonished to find itself on his itinerary and in such splendid company. It had attracted his attention by its conduct towards him and many of his friends during the austere postwar years. The village school at Abinger had been adopted and sent pencils and crayons and copybooks. Professors and students had been introduced to suitable English friends. Letters and little gifts flew or floated back and forth. Morgan came to say thank you.

The rest of his trip took him to Bryn Mawr College, where he read portions of his books; to the Grand Canyon, which he had the stamina to descend on mule back; to Boulder Dam, to Los Angeles, where he saw his old friends, Gerald Heard, Christopher Isherwood, and Christopher Wood; to San Francisco and the Yosemite Valley and to Chicago. He saw and absorbed more of us than do most foreign travellers.

In June he came back to Tyringham, staying this time at the Lost Farm. It is so called because the house is visible on its little rise of land from the valley road but, when you go along the roads which would seem to lead to it, they lead past instead, and you are back in the valley looking over at it again. Its secret is that the road on which it was built in the mid-eighteenth century was abandoned about a hundred years ago and now the house sits in the midst of its land . . . over a hundred acres of woods and fields and marsh, not aloof, but alone and reclusive. Its name appears in the dedication of *Two Cheers for Democracy*, so I shall describe it further.

It is a wooden house of the kind which we call a salt-box because of its long sloping back roof which comes down on to the first storey. The front part is two storeys high. It has a central chimney, which held up the structure during its period of extreme neglect. Morgan's room was in the north-east corner, with a view of the valley from one window and of a white lilac tree from the others. It had rather sketchy, unpainted walls, a brass bedstead and a fireplace. It had a beamed ceiling which once was white but was now stained by the rain and melting snow. They had free access for some years before my ownership. I had managed to prevent their entry into this room, but the stains remained and Morgan enjoyed them. They looked like elephants and deer and horses and people. He urged me not to whiten the ceiling and spoil the fun of waking up to those shiftable images.

The long, cool living-room had a wall of books. The large kitchen in which one ate, smoked, drank, talked, and sat about had a coal-oil stove. There was a terrace off this, facing south-west, and much time was spent there soaking up the summer sun. There was no telephone, electricity or plumbing.

Morgan's chore was to bring up two pails of water from the brook each morning for the morning coffee and ablutions. These latter occurred out of doors with the aid of an enamel basin. Serious bathing, if at all, occurred in the swimming-hole in the Hop Brook, which runs or ambles along one edge of the property. A bar of soap was kept there in a coffee tin, so that the resident beasts wouldn't chew it before the guests had a chance to use it. Morgan said that the place reminded him of Clouds Hill. I had not then read his essay on T. E. Lawrence's house (TC, 352–5) and did not know what a compliment he paid the farm. His admonition was: "Don't let the ladies make it cottagey-chintzy. They will want to." I'm afraid that they did and have. In those days it was sketchy, uncomfortable, but somehow comforting.

Thanks to the half-washed-out carriage road which provided the only approach to the house, we were not greatly bothered with visitors. When on one occasion we were, we heard a car bouncing through the woods in time to hide in the shrubbery, thus avoiding an important and curious county family.

I had to leave Morgan alone one evening. The kerosene lamps had Welsbach mantles and gave a bright enough light for reading, but were moody and apt to burn irregularly, sooting up their mantles, then their chimneys and finally the entire room. All three degrees of sooting had in turn occurred to all three lamps. So, although Morgan had started happily enough reading Cavafy's poems, which he had found among my father's books, he was reduced, finally, to one candle and then to retiring. His only diversion, apart from the occasional scratching of a branch against the house, was the hoot of the owl, the scampering of mice in the attic and the occasional velvet intrusion of a bat. He did not mind.

I sometimes wish that children were not allowed to read the story about the princess and the pea. I think that it is a bad story. It gives the impression that fussing over personal comfort is a sign of nobility. I think that it is even an untrue story and that a princess would spend the night on a mattress full of peas and in the morning say: "How kind of you to have let me stay." That is certainly Morgan's form of politeness and, if it is not the way in which nobility behaves, then it is the way in which they should, if a member of a democracy may be allowed to dictate.

Morgan came again to America in May of 1949 at the invitation of the Academy of Arts and Letters. He spoke to them on "Art for Art's Sake". This time he brought with him, to our great delight, his closest friend, Bob Buckingham.

They stayed, while in New York, at 5 St. Luke's Place in a flat which the painter, Jared French, lent them. One evening when Morgan, Bob, and I were walking through Times Square we met, by happy accident, Hank Henry, the burlesque comedian, whom they had seen in *This Is the Army* at the Palladium during the war. "All the burlesque houses in New York have been padlocked. I've got to work in Jersey. Why don't you come over and see me?" They did and were delighted with the strippers, bumpers, grinders, and Hank's more than music-hall bawdiness.

They visited Glenway Wescott and his family at Stone Blossom, New Jersey; they stayed with the Edward Roots in Clinton, N.Y., while Morgan accepted an honorary degree from Hamilton College. They spent a few days at Bethayres, Pennsylvania, with Tom Coley and his mother in a house whose wide veranda and overgrown lush gardens reminded Morgan of India; and where the huge, rare roast beef reminded him of pre-war England. They went to Washington, D.C., and they came to the Lost Farm. The visit there was shorter than the first, and it was Morgan's last.

On both trips to America I tried to protect Morgan's privacy from invasion so long as he was with me. I was not always successful. There was one determined lady who wanted to persuade Morgan to write something for publication. "Any little impression. Even a letter!" He twice politely fended her off. But she was determined. I was about to jump into the conversation to protect him when my usually gentle friend became briefly formidable. He fixed her with a firm, arresting look. "I have tried to tell you this twice, but you seem not to have heard. Will you attend? I have no intention of writing anything while I am in America. Were I to do so, it would not be published by your company. Now, may we talk of something else?" I thought: "And this is the defenceless creature whom I felt I had to protect?" I was delighted. It is the only time I have seen the flash of his teeth, but then it is also the only time I have seen him treated like, and so turned into, a lion.

Later I apologised for the fact that the lady had gotten through my guard. He was amused. "I have been meeting that lady for years. When I was a very small frog in a very small pond she came out from Dorking to get me to write little pieces for the local newspaper. Now that I am a rather large frog in a very large pond she comes from New York. She is always the same lady." Then he added: "No, to give her her due, this one is the best of her breed."

For the most part, the personal encounters here were a success. Many people, known and acknowledged, unknown and unnameable, have contributed to Morgan's happiness and pleasure and productivity. Lest some of the anonymous Americans be overlooked, I mention the farmer with whom he discussed the advantages of bringing up children in the country, the farm woman who had saved him two duck eggs to cook for his breakfast, and the neighbouring field hands who would drop in to sit with him in front of the kitchen fire. There was also the waitress who said: "Oh, don't order that, sir! They make it on Monday and we have to eat it all week." And the conductor on the train with whom Morgan traded maps of New York City. The conductor liked Morgan's map because it gave newer information. Morgan preferred the conductor's because it had larger print. The exchange ended with Morgan's being helped politely down the train steps, slapped heartily on the back, and told to "Take it easy, sir!"

Little scenes like this caused Morgan to say that Americans have beautiful manners. I protested that this was truer of the English, but Morgan insisted that the English politeness was habit: the country being smaller and the concentration of people higher, it was necessary that a good many "Thank yous" and "Tas" and "So sorrys" be muttered to avoid irritation and anger. He contended that they were uttered with no awareness of the person to whom they were said, and were hence not truly polite. Our brash non-etiquette pleased him more because he claimed we connected more.

One evening in a restaurant in New York Morgan tried to pay for four of us. He had his wallet out and was saying "Please let me" when Tom Coley said: "Drop dead, Forster, I'm paying this!" Morgan laughed and dropped his wallet. It was probably the first time he had heard "drop dead", which was a current expression. What made him laugh, though, was the contradiction of insult and kindness in one slangy sweep. Tom had won.

Morgan is, of course, the final winner. His generosity is prodigious to all of his friends. Tom and I, on visits to England, have received theatre tickets, train tickets, meals, lodging, even bits of money left in envelopes containing jokey notes pretending to be from celebrated stars or fictitious characters, anyone but Morgan.

When we were both younger and I had less understanding, I used to badger Morgan in an effort to get him to write more. I once told him of an acquaintance of mine who had to move away from his mistress in order to get back to writing. "But," said Morgan, "my mistresses are procrastination and sloth!" He later ended a letter to me with: "My mistresses send their love."

I was still at him about writing when he came to America. Morgan was firm. "But I've said what I have to say in the only ways I can think of. One of the reasons I'm glad to have done the *Raison d'Etre* is that it gave me a chance to say it again, in relation to criticism and the approach to the arts. And I have only one thing to say." "What is that?" "You know . . . love." I said that I had feared he might have lost the urge to fall in love with new ideas. "Oh, no!" said Morgan. "I hope that I shall be able to fall in love with a new idea on my death-bed."

Morgan noted little things about us. He was pleased by our habit of saying "You're welcome" when thanked. Years later the Patrick Wilkinsons' children were heard playing at being American. They ran about repeating: "You're welcome, you're welcome!" He noticed, too, that we, possibly the least relaxed of people, constantly use the word "Relax!" as a command.

Something of his private voice is caught in his book inscriptions. There was a copy of *Howards End* on the shelves at the Lost Farm. Morgan found it and wrote above my signature on the fly-leaf: "E. M. Forster wishes he had given this to . . ." In the published version of Santha Rama Rau's dramatisation of *A Passage to India*, he wrote: "Tom, with Morgan's love, who didn't write it. But what of that."

Of his letters, I find the following relevant. To my sister, in

June of 1949, he wrote from Bethayres, where he and Bob were staying with Tom Coley:

> You should have been having a lovely week-end at Tyringham. I always feel so happy there and feel its countryside is real country. This place and Stone Blossom, N. J. are charming in their various ways but they have the organising touch of the city on them, whereas the Berkshires exist on their own . . . Lost Farm particularly. My love to your mother. I hope she enjoyed it [her trip to the Farm]. Also Minky, whom Tom has just had the unkindness to call an animated lizard. I have had a wonderful time on the whole. I started sneezing at a dinner at the Century Club . . . the atmosphere was one of high compliment . . . they said how wonderful I was, I said how wonderful they were, and every now and then sneezed. Please excuse bad writing . . . am upon a sofa. I think I hear the bathers returning. Yes, I hear the yap of the Pennsylvania Minky [Tom's dog] who is called Junior or June-June and is large and white.

Then on 10 August 1961 came a letter in which occurred:

> Delighted too . . . at this point one person after another came in, and I have forgotten what delighted me. I go to Aldeburgh tomorrow and later in the month, as you have already been advised, to St. Remy. I have now remembered what also delighted me: your joint descent of the Grand Canyon, complete with photos and my own membership of the BUM BUMPERS CLUB.

This last refers to a certificate issued to all who make the mule trip down the canyon and back. Morgan had failed to get his documentation at the time of his own trip and we got it for him.

Tom and I had to drive in tandem in two cars from Los Angeles to New York, starting out the morning after President Kennedy was assassinated. Morgan wrote to Tom on 20 December 1963:

> So you had to drive across a whole continent at that appalling time. I can think of no strain more terrible. It is *the* worst thing that could happen for America and the world. People will settle down, of course, and resume their company director smiles. But

the main turning towards safety has been lost. Many individuals, though, will never forget. I am still wearing mourning tie, which I have never done or wished to do before.

On 22 May 1964 he wrote the following from Cambridge:

We have had about five days of adorable weather, something beyond belief, in which butterflies skipped around. Grey skies have now returned but different sorts of green still gloam. Unfortunately I forget everything at once, but do not cease in general admiration and gratitude.

It is not a bad place to leave him, reminding us to admire and be grateful.

This has been a lapsing memoir. Were I able to read it with a clear and disconnected eye, I am sure I could point out that it lacks form. Perhaps, though, it has managed to say Love at the beginning, in the middle, and at the end.

Forster as a Humanist

by W. J. H. Sprott

Before I begin I ought to declare an interest. Forster has been not only a friend, but a guide as well. Ever since I met him in the 1920s he has been the most influential person in my life. I mention this because I must necessarily write about him from my own personal point of view, and may therefore present a picture which will be unrecognisable to many people, and, I may add, to Forster himself. This is unavoidable. However, I am saved from complete misrepresentation by his own words, particularly those collected together in *Two Cheers for Democracy*.

When Forster stopped writing novels he became a sage. This was not, of course, taking on another occupation, like a plumber becoming a bricklayer; sagacity was there from the start. For me the fascination of his fiction lies not so much in the stories themselves as in the comments he makes about the characters and their confrontations. Since the publication in 1924 of *A Passage to India*, however, he has expressed his views in a more direct form. This is what I mean by saying that he became a sage, a word which I fear he may not like, but I can think of no other.

In 1945 while he was in India, I was looking after his mail, when two letters arrived, one from solicitors naming a date for him to leave his home at Abinger, and another from the Provost of King's offering him an Honorary Fellowship with residence in the College. I retained the first—why should he be bothered?—and sent the second to him.

Thus it came about that since 1945 he has lived at Cambridge as an Honorary Fellow of King's. He has been among friends who are devoted to him, and in addition he has enjoyed a notable success with the young. Of course they are drawn by his fame as a novelist, of course they are captivated by his charm and his diffidence—he is always genuinely astonished that anyone should pay the slightest attention to him. Celebrity and charm have played their part in attracting the young, and other people for that matter. But that is not the whole story. The young have recognised him as a wise man. He is receptive to their views; they enjoy his comments, which so often accord with their own ideas. No wonder that he has been a leading member of the Cambridge Humanist movement.

What is a humanist? In a short paragraph in the *Encyclopaedia Britannica*, eleventh edition, we read: "Humanism (from Lat. *humanus*, human, connected with *homo*, mankind): in general, any system of thought or action which assigns a predominant interest to the affairs of men as compared with the supernatural or the abstract." The *Encyclopaedia of the Social Sciences* goes into the matter at greater length, tracing the movement back to the discovery of the literature of Greece and Rome in the Renaissance, when the hold of dogmatic religion was weakening. A new world was opening up, which the intelligentsia found entrancing. "Man is the measure of all things," they learned from Protagoras. The movement began in Italy, in cities where commerce flourished and at luxurious courts. "Only in a consumers' civilisation such as the Italian," we are told, "founded on wealth and leisure, could such a movement take place." This, of course, was written by a sociologist, and, although Forster would doubtless accept it, he would do so with a sigh; he does not care for money-making or commerce, and it is perhaps a little paradoxical that the ideas which he espouses should have had their roots in this uncongenial atmosphere.

Forster himself has characterised humanism in writing about
Gide (TC, 233). "The humanist," he says, "has four leading
characteristics—curiosity, a free mind, belief in good taste, and
belief in the human race." How does Forster make out on these
criteria?

Curiosity? I have to admit that before reading these words I
had not thought of Forster as particularly curious, but on reflection I realise that I was wrong. His range of literary criticism displays an inquiring mind. He ranges with ease from William Barnes
to d'Annunzio. He is curious about music. He is curious about
places, in the sense that wherever he goes he is sensitive to their
distinctive features and to any oddities which present themselves.
When it comes to people, his curiosity is, I think, a little hampered
by his standards. He dislikes anything that smells of grandeur, he
shrinks from it and may miss something of interest as a result.
One rather unusual subject about which he is curious is the
functioning, or, more accurately, the malfunctioning, of his body.
He has had several disturbing bouts of illness, and has borne them
all with a courage that takes, as one of its forms, that of interested
detachment. When he is on the mend he will tell the sympathiser
about his symptoms, and the doctors' efforts at curing them, as
though amused at contemplating what he has been through. If
you exclaim "Oh, Morgan, how awful . . ." his reply will most
likely be: "Well, it was rather peculiar." On one occasion he lost
his power of speech. Suddenly it came back, and his hostess, who
is a nurse, was astonished to hear him say "Good morning" in the
most cheerful tone. I asked him about this experience. Had he
known what he wanted to say, but been unable to say it? "Yes,
indeed," he told me, "it was most amusing. I used to laugh, and
they" (his host and hostess) "would laugh, too, but I expect it
was out of politeness." On another occasion he was talking about
the disposition of his affairs on his death. He was so cheerful about
it that I ventured to ask him what he would wish done as some
kind of memorial ceremony. No Christian burial, of course; I
knew that. But King's College would wish to do something. What
about a concert in the Chapel? "Oh no, not the *Chapel*; that would

smell too much of religion. It would be letting the humanists down." I apologised for discussing a rather lugubrious subject. "Not at all, it is *most* interesting." Yes, no doubt about it: he passes his own test of curiosity.

The second characteristic of Forster's humanist is "a free mind". There can be no question about this qualification. Forster has a free-ranging intellect, an unfailing readiness to consider new ideas, and a complete disregard for authority.

We pass on to his third criterion: "belief in good taste". Again there is no question. The phrasing of the criterion, however, is significant. He does not say that the humanist must *have* good taste, but that he must *believe* in it. He may possess it also, but who is to judge its "goodness"? What is required is that he should value discrimination. The works of man are varied, and different people have their lives enriched by different things. What is important is that people should recognise what enriches their lives from what does not, and should help others to find their sources of enrichment. Agreement is irrelevant. What I have said concerns the world of the arts, but a belief in discrimination is even more important in another field—the broad field of human institutions and behaviour. We must discriminate between the good and the bad, and denounce the latter with boldness. It is this belief in taste that plays a vital part in Forster's position on the fourth criterion.

The fourth criterion is "belief in the human race". Here we meet with difficulties. In a sense, once religion is abandoned, the human race and its potentialities are all we have to believe in. It has remarkable achievements to its credit, but there is much that is, to say the least, discreditable and hampering. This is where discrimination comes in.

Forster, I think, would agree (though he would not express himself in such prosaic terms) that one achievement of the human race has been the establishment and progressive refinement of a standard of moral values. The conventional view that moral standards are derived from religion is the reverse of the truth. Human interaction requires a system of mutual expectations, and the expected behaviours of any culture are given sanctification by the current religious beliefs. Indeed, as we have seen in recent years, religious sanctification is a mixed blessing; it holds up moral advance. This achievement in the moral field is one which marks us off from the other animals. It is in terms of these moral standards that the discrimination between good and bad behaviour is made.

A second achievement of the human race is the production of works of art. For Forster this is, perhaps, its greatest achievement. In his lecture on "Art for Art's Sake" he contrasts the disorder of everyday life with the order of a work of art, which "stands up by itself" (TC, 101). He asserts

> not only the existence of art, but its pertinacity. Looking back into the past, it seems to me that that is all there has ever been: vantage grounds for discussion and creation, little vantage grounds in the changing chaos, where bubbles have been blown and webs spun, and the desire to create order has found temporary gratification. (p. 103.)

In the essay on "Anonymity" he thinks of a work of art as anonymous. The artist, and perhaps everyone to some degree, has two personalities. There is the "upper" personality of everyday life, and there is the "lower" personality, "in the obscure recesses of our being", down into which the artist dips a bucket (an image frequently used by Forster), and out of which he creates a work of art. (TC, 93.)

But the creation of works of art requires propitious conditions. The essay on "Art for Art's Sake" contains these words: "What I hope for today is a disorder which will be more favourable to artists than is the present one, and which will provide them with fuller inspirations and better material conditions." (TC, 99.)

So the human race has produced individuals of moral worth and works of art. When I say "individuals of moral worth", I do not mean saints of spectacular virtue. By no manner of means. Forster would no doubt include them, but his taste is for simple, kindly, unpretentious people. If they are intelligent, this is all to the good, because they enliven conversation, but it is not important to him. Warmth of character is what really matters.

Furthermore it is the individual and not mankind that he cares about. "I have no mystic faith in the people. I have in the individual. He seems to me a divine achievement and I mistrust any view which belittles him." (TC, 68.) This comes out more emphatically in "What I Believe". "Where do I start?" he asks. "With personal relationships." (TC, 77.) And later (p. 78) he makes that celebrated statement: "I hate the idea of causes, and if I had to choose between betraying my country and betraying my friend, I hope I should have the guts to betray my country." But individuals must be given a chance to develop their potentialities, whether for creating works of art, or making scientific discoveries, or being "creative in their private lives". This is where democracy comes in. "All these people need to express themselves; they cannot do so unless society allows them liberty to do so, and the society which allows them most liberty is a democracy . . . . So Two cheers for Democracy." (p. 79.)

In the gloom he detects "an aristocracy of the sensitive, the considerate and the plucky . . . . With this type of person knocking about, and constantly crossing one's path if one has eyes to see or hands to feel, the experiment of earthly life cannot be dismissed as a failure." (pp. 82–3.)

Thus Forster's belief in the human race is discriminating. It has potentialities, it is not a failure, but there are defects which hamper the realisation of its possibilities. These defects can, I think, be divided into two classes. On the one hand there are defects in human nature itself—"original sins", one might say, though Forster might well dislike the expression on account of its connotations. On the other hand, and perhaps more sinister, there are impediments built into human society.

The defects of human nature are obvious enough—cruelty, selfishness, lack of consideration, and so on. Forster does not explicitly concern himself with these; his disapproval is implied by his praise of their opposites. The defects he does castigate are power-mongering and pretentiousness. "If . . . men were more interested in knowledge than in power, mankind would be in a far safer position." (TC, 100.) Power-mongering is a serious danger; pretentiousness is scarcely that, but Forster finds it deeply distasteful. This comes out again and again in the novels, and in the rather cruel deflation of Mrs. Miniver, with her easy manners, her amusing chatter, her belief that she comes out of the top drawer, when really it is "the top drawer but one . . . . She has her own style, but she has not Style." (TC, 306.) He sometimes takes his distaste for pretentiousness a little far. He once took me to luncheon at a celebrated restaurant in London. He wanted me to have a good time, as he always does with his friends. We had hardly sat down at our table when he started intermittent mutterings. The service was bad, the food inferior, the décor hideous. He was not rude, of course, he is the politest of men, but he thought the place too pretentious by half, and with all its pretentiousness it was really second-rate. I need hardly say that the meat and two veg. at a workman's café was invariably found to be delicious.

On another occasion, when I was staying with him in his London flat, he was suddenly taken ill. The doctor was sent for and told him to stay in bed until he called next day. Forster was particularly anxious to get back to Cambridge on the following day, and I suggested that if the doctor allowed it he could have a car. "Oh, but that would be very extravagant," he said; and in the event he did not even take the taxi to the station which the doctor had stipulated. The most generous of men to his friends, Forster dislikes spending money on himself; but my reason for telling this story is that taking a car all the way from London to Cambridge would, in Forster's eyes, have been pretentious.

The second type of impediment to mankind's full development is concerned with the organisation of society. Society is a muddled affair, as we have seen, but it is not all muddle. Efforts are made to organise the muddle, and these, though doubtless necessary, are often disastrous. Writing just after the Second World War he says:

> The doctrine of *laissez-faire* will not work in the material world. It has led to the black market and the capitalist jungle. We must have planning and ration books and controls . . . . On the other hand, the doctrine of *laissez-faire* is the only one that seems to work in the world of the spirit. (TC, 68.)

And this system of controls grows increasingly necessary as the economic world becomes more complex with the development of large-scale industry.

> It has meant organisation and plans and the boosting of the community. It has meant the destruction of feudalism and relationship based on the land, it has meant the transference of power from the aristocrat to the bureaucrat and the manager and the technician. Perhaps it will mean democracy, but it has not meant it yet, and personally I hate it. (p. 281.)

And in addition you have divided loyalties:

> When there is a collision of principles, would you favour the individual at the expense of the community as I would? Or would you prefer economic justice for all at the expense of personal freedom? (p. 69.)

And what can one do? An artist "ought to express what he wants and not what he is told to express by the planning authorities" (p. 70). But there is something more he can do. He can protest. It does not do much good, but it is something. That is why Forster was for many years a prominent member of the National Council for Civil Liberties. He says he hates causes, but this is not quite true. Protection of civil liberties, and protestation when they are infringed, is a cause which he has espoused—though in a sense it is a cause to protect people against causes.

Writing during the Second World War, in 1941, he is anxious about our behaviour to the Germans when it is over. He pleads for tolerance: "Don't try to love them: you can't, you'll only strain yourself. But try to tolerate them." (TC, 56–7.) This plea for tolerance extends far beyond the context in which it was written; it applies to us all, at all times, when confronted with people we cannot love.

Some Notes on Forster and Music

by Benjamin Britten

There is no doubt that E. M. Forster is our most musical novelist. And I don't mean that he just likes music or likes going to concerts and operas, or plays the piano neatly and efficiently (all of which he does), but that he really understands music and uses music in his novels, and fairly frequently. The musical *locus classicus* is, of course, in *Howards End* (pp. 32–6) where a number of characters are presented in a tiny musical vignette—each of them reacting in a different way to a performance of Beethoven's Fifth Symphony. Musically they range from Mrs. Munt, who wants to tap "surreptitiously", via Fräulein Mosebach, who is reminded that it is "echt Deutsch", Helen who sees pictures in it (goblins and elephants), and Margaret who just listens, to Tibby (poor Tibby!) who is up in the techniques of of music and "implored the company generally to look out for the transitional passage on the drum". The whole remarkable passage shows a most sensitive reaction to music, and allows the novelist to make some perceptive observations on Beethoven—profound enough to help explain why his music has kept its hold on the public's affection all these years: ". . . the goblins were there. They could return. He had said so bravely, and that is why one can trust Beethoven when he says other things." The passage also allows him to make some less valid observations on the acoustics of the lamented Queen's Hall, which make curious reading when one thinks of the acoustics and general concert atmosphere of the South Bank complex. The science of acoustics does not seem to have advanced much in the last half-century. Concerts in the Queen's Hall were a joy to hear; big and small music came winging to one with real resonance; the sounds were not dry or boxy.

In *A Room with a View* Lucy Honeychurch seems an inhibited, muddled little person until she is heard playing the piano by Mr. Beebe. Both her playing and her choice of music—especially the choice of Beethoven's opus 111 for "one of those entertainments where the upper classes entertain the lower" (p. 41)—have previously surprised him, and now surprise us. But Forster knows his Beethoven sonatas (which I have heard him play with spirit), and he selects the music carefully. No wonder Mr. Beebe was "disturbed".

Forster certainly remembers his own piano-duet playing, and those painful collisions which skin the little fingers, in the music lessons which start the short story "Co-ordination". Again the pupils play Beethoven, and the dreadful ring of their names, Mildred and Ellen, Rose and Enid, Margaret and Jane, Dolores and Violet, echoes their dreadful thumping—it is hardly surprising that their teacher is at the end of her tether. Beethoven in heaven is concerned with the totting up of his performances, but still being deaf is deceived by his clerk about their quality. One wonders what the girls would have made of their celestial reward—a performance of his A minor quartet; what they actually hear is a brass band (more their cup of tea!).

Music is used superbly, not so much to colour a character as to push on the action, towards the end of *Where Angels Fear to Tread*. Here one may perhaps observe that the construction of Forster's novels often resembles that of the "classical" opera (Mozart—Weber—Verdi) where recitatives (the deliberately un-lyrical passages by which the action is advanced) separate arias or ensembles (big, self-contained set pieces of high comedy or great emotional tension). As examples of the latter, think of the bathing episode in *A Room with a View*, the school Sunday dinner at which Ansell confronts Rickie in *The Longest Journey*, and, perhaps greatest of all, the trial in *A Passage to India*. The purpose of the big musical episode in *Where Angels Fear to Tread* is to dent deeper Philip Herriton's defences by confronting him with Gino at his gayest and most ingenuous. The scene, *Lucia di Lammermoor* at the Monteriano opera house, is long and gloriously funny: the fat lady of the railway journey "who had never, never before . . ." turning up as the prima donna; Harriet trying to stop an Italian audience from talking, and trying to follow the plot; the triumph of the Mad Scene with the clothes-horse of flowers; and the cries of "Let the divine creature continue". But, as always with Forster (as with Mozart, too), under the comedy lies seriousness, passion, and warmth: the warmth of the Italians loving their tunes, being relaxed and gay together, and not being afraid of showing their feelings—not "pretending", like Sawston.

Outside his novels and stories, Forster has written three important essays about music: "The C Minor of That Life" (TC, 132–5), "Not Listening to Music" (TC, 136–9), and a broadcast talk, "Revolution at Bayreuth" (*The Listener*, 4 November 1954, pp. 755–7). The Aldeburgh lecture "George Crabbe and Peter Grimes" (TC, 178–92) only mentions music in passing; it is really about Crabbe's feelings, very involved ones, towards the town of Aldeburgh, and contains a long and detailed analysis of the poem. The Harvard lecture, "The *Raison d'Etre* of Criticism in the Arts" (TC, 117–31), does not deal specifically with music, except once, again in connection with Beethoven.

The first of these essays, "The C Minor of That Life", bravely tackles a technical problem which has baffled musicians ever since "tempered tuning" came in. Is there actually a difference in character between keys other than highness or lowness—for instance, is it just arbitrary that composers go pastoral in F, sensual in F sharp, stern and fateful in C minor, and so on? Without going too much into technical details, it is scientifically provable that, since tempered tuning has changed the intervals between the notes, the common chords of the different keys, and their scales, are slightly differently spaced, and so have slightly different characters. Apart from this physical aspect there is, of course, that of association, and this Forster does realise: because Beethoven has written some very memorable pieces in C minor, C minor has for us a special quality. The essay has some other acute observations, one inaccuracy (perhaps intentional?—there are no movements in C minor in the Razumovsky quartets), and a little jibe at Mozart.

"Revolution at Bayreuth" is Forster at his musical best. He writes wisely about Wagner, his music, our different attitudes to it (although I could quarrel with his calling his orchestration "thick"), his qualities as a dramatist, and the interpretation of his extravagant stage directions. It is, of course, the attitude of the present "Reich" at Bayreuth which started off the essay and justifies its title. I hope this most valuable piece of musical Forster will soon become more easily available.

"Not Listening to Music" is again amusing and acute, but in it there is the same curious tendency to mock at any intellectual approach on the part of the listener which we have noticed once or twice before. Thus in *Howards End* the novelist is determined to paint Tibby black, or dark grey—a determination which I do not think succeeds, since I can't help reacting sympathetically to the boy and want to know more about him—and one of the ways of doing this is to make him "intellectual" about music, and therefore not "feel" it; it is "dangerous" to know a lot about it. In "Not Listening to Music" we are told that no one can listen to a piece of music from beginning to end, consistently—unless one is a "professional critic". The alternatives to listening include watching the conductor, or the singer with her chin or chins, and noting the extreme ugliness of the audience (is this true?); and, of course, when one returns to the music, there are the pictorial images—the hunting scenes, Orpheus and the Furies (and Helen's elephants and goblins), in fact anything but the music itself. In "The *Raison d'Etre* of Criticism" he refers to the Choral Symphony "in A", when a reference book or catalogue would easily have put him right; his wistful "Isn't it in A?" seems to suggest that this is a deliberate misnomer. No, for some reason Forster does not want to admit that knowing about music is a help: Tibby should not bother about such things as transitional passages. But surely no one pretends that to know this is all-important, any more than Helen's goblins are. Why does he take this attitude? It can be summed up in his attitude to Mozart, the Mozart who, "in this respect [the use of a particular key for a particular mood], and indeed in others . . . did not go so far" as Beethoven: the Mozart whom I have heard him call "tinkling".[1] Simply, Forster prefers music based on striking themes, dramatic happenings, and strong immediate moods, rather than on classical control and balance, beautiful melodies and perfection of detail; music which benefits from being listened to closely and from some knowledge of it. He prefers the Romantic to the Classical. And why shouldn't he?— he was brought up musically at the end of the nineteenth century. This is, of course, an overstatement, because, in spite of the pendulum swinging sharply away from Romanticism today, Forster *is* interested in new music—I have heard him react sympathetically to Stravinsky, to Michael Tippett, and also to some of my own pieces.

So when, in the late 1940s, having the deepest admiration for his writing, I suggested our doing an opera together, he agreed happily. At the start he was characteristically timid about it, worried by his lack of experience. But when Eric Crozier agreed to collaborate, with his considerable operatic background, he felt more confident—if we could find a mutually acceptable subject. We each suggested subjects, nearly settling on the Suffolk story *Margaret Catchpole*, but not quite. Who brought up the idea of *Billy Budd* no one can quite remember; it was probably telepathic and simultaneous. I think the writing of the libretto gave him great pleasure. Certainly the summer of 1950, when he stayed for a long time at Aldeburgh, when the sun seemed to shine continuously and we would go out for relaxation in a boat with a fisherman friend (curiously resembling the Billy we were writing about), was my own happiest operatic collaboration. Naturally

[1] Lucy Honeychurch was found by Mr. Beebe on one occasion "tinkling at a Mozart Sonata" (RV, 219).

Forster and Broadcasting

by John Arlott

During the Second World War the B.B.C., within its Eastern Service, built up a programme-grouping called "English to India" which was of a uniformly higher cultural and intellectual standard than any other section of British broadcasting until the creation of the Third Programme. It was not directly propagandist, but it sought, like much of the B.B.C.'s overseas output of the war period, to establish sympathy for Britain by its quality and integrity. It had the advantage that it could attract an audience beyond the confines of India—among English-speaking people in Burma and Malaya—but it was never intended to be majority listening. It was aimed at the influential minority, the relatively wealthy who possessed short-wave sets and were prepared to listen perseveringly despite the irritations of that form of reception, who were educated to university standard and felt a need for programmes uncompromisingly directed at that level. There is much evidence that it was successful in its aim.

When, after the war, I took over from George Orwell as literary programmes producer in the Eastern Service, I inherited a weekly half-hour poetry programme, a weekly quarter-hour on English prose-writing, and a monthly book review by E. M. Forster. Forster was the one contributor the programme *had* to have if it was to command respect in India. He accepted that fact and became its only regular contributor throughout the war and for some three years afterwards. Often, in conversation with Indians, one found almost staggering evidence of the respect in which Forster is held in their country, and of the immense prestige the B.B.C. gained from the fact that he was broadcasting in its service to India.

He did not do these broadcasts for the usual reasons: he was not concerned with what he might earn from them, and he had neither the need nor the wish to create a reputation as a broadcaster. He did, in fact, broadcast with great success from time to time, over a thirty-year period, in the B.B.C.'s domestic programmes; but his enthusiasm was reserved for his talks to India—or, more precisely, to Indians. His strongest motive was his liking for Indians: when he was in India he preferred the company of Indians to that of English people, and he usually travelled second class on trains, mixing happily with Indians, strangers to him, who happened to be in the carriage. He was as eager as *A Passage to India* would suggest to establish understanding, trust, and affection between Indians and people like himself. At a slightly lower level, he was anxious to show Indians that people like himself did exist in Britain. He was aware also that the broadcasting, to India, of good English speech was in itself valuable. He recognised—without pressing the point, for he was completely conscious of the quality of much literature in the native languages, especially Bengali—the value and possibilities of English as a common literary language in a multilingual country. He perceived, too, that often, for social reasons which distressed him, too many Indians were learning bad or indifferent English because they learned it only from other Indians. So, for various reasons, it was his wish and, as he saw it, his duty, to speak in English to Indians.

His monthly, quarter-hour talk was labelled a book review, but in essence it was a personal talk, a friendly and at the same time scholarly communication delivered with considerable, if unemphasised, skill. His script arrived regularly, hand-written on pages from old—usually slightly discoloured—exercise books. His handwriting gave unusual difficulty, even to secretaries accustomed to copying manuscript material, and, although he had the helpful habit of beginning proper nouns with block capitals, he tended to lose patience with a word of any length, and brush rather shapelessly through its last three or four letters. It was not until I had been consulted a number of times to identify words that the source of the problem dawned on me: he did not use the usual word, or the cliché, but attempted always to *define*. The first word that made this clear to me was "formalism"—I recall the word, but not the context. The next was "the *discrepancies* of human nature". Neither word was, in point of fact, ill written; but both were unexpected.

He used to come to the studio on a convenient afternoon to record his talk. In winter he would appear in a long, rather worn overcoat, and a heavy woollen scarf, carefully safety-pinned across his chest and not to be removed, even in a centrally heated studio. Initially and briefly he would seem wary, but he relaxed quickly into conversational certainty, with his characteristic, and often disconcerting, switches from the coolly objective to the completely unguarded subjective. He needed little production of the usual kind. As Orwell told me, "Forster is no work at all; but don't try to alter him." His time-length—the constant problem with non-professional broadcasters—was rarely wrong by more than a few seconds; and at times a considerable weight of alterations indicated the care he had taken over his script.

His broadcasts had much of the quality of his writing, of complete, terse thoughts producing a cumulative effect. There was the same limpid clarity, the same capacity to arrest with simple words simply arranged, the same ability to capture the characteristics of other people's speech, and to speak in his own word-patterns. Since, however, his usual style would have been too concentrated for good listening, he consciously diluted it with the throw-away phrase, often the deliberate colloquialism or the personal note which suited his voice so well: he would introduce a point with "I want to talk—or rather to chat—about . . ." When, on the other hand, the rhythm of a sentence demanded a more formal word, he would say, for example: "I shall conclude with . . ."

He liked to use a producer as a sample listener and, again unlike many who come to broadcasting as a sideline, he listened to every suggestion as a basis for discussion. Once, at the hint that there should be a longer pause between two words, he altered a comma to a semi-colon, for his punctuation reflected his intended delivery. On another occasion, when it seemed to me that the antithetical relationship between two sentences needed to be brought out more clearly, he asked: "What word do you suggest I put in?" "But," I said. "No, no, I don't like it: 'but' is a lazy man's word—used instead of the proper word—no, I think I'll say 'on the other hand'."

At first hearing his voice seemed flat and lacking in character. It was, however, clear, and, perhaps most important of all, it was marked by a quality which is much rarer than might be supposed, by the wish to communicate, by conscious awareness that he was speaking to listeners. He had obviously been warned of the problems of long-range, short-wave broadcasting, and he concentrated on clarity, and rarely hurried. So his variations were slight, but they were controlled and effective and, when he touched on the objects of his disapprobation, he could sound quite startlingly steely and implacable.

Once, when none of the latest books interested him, he began with a discussion of writing during war or its aftermath, in the course of which he used the longest sentence I ever heard from him: "In the region of the spirit there is doubt and withdrawal and mistrust of the cries of the planners, plan they never so lordly, and this doubt and withdrawal impairs artistic work at the source, and prevents visions from taking an external form, to the profit and delight of mankind." The separation, by voice, of the first "doubt and withdrawal" from "mistrust of the cries of the planners", the heightened parenthesis of "plan they never so lordly", the repetition of "doubt and withdrawal" and the effective fall of "the profit and delight of mankind" are all examples of quite masterly writing for speech; and he spoke it with unusual and moving vehemence.

He could be immensely subtle, as when, in a talk about Tolstoy, pegged somewhat tenuously to the novelist's birthday, he used as the last sentence of one paragraph and the first of the next "Let us celebrate his birthday" and "Let's celebrate him as a writer of short stories." The distinction between "Let us" and "Let's" and the use of "a writer of short stories" instead of "a short-story writer" are the mark of a man who writes by ear and, which is not the same thing, to be heard.

There is no doubt that he appreciated the integrity of the B.B.C. as reflected by Orwell, but also that he was constantly on the alert against the forces of reaction which might destroy that integrity, and restrict the freedom of broadcasters like himself. Once, in a talk, he passed what seemed to me harsh comment on a writer for whom I had a warm personal feeling. After the run-through I suggested a modification of the criticism. He looked at me quite coldly and said: "That is what I think about him and that is what I want to say about him." He said it.

His broadcasts were creative and valuable both in their own right and in their value to the B.B.C. For many years, too, he made them with obvious pleasure; but eventually there was an obvious decline in his enthusiasm, and I was not surprised when he wrote, courteously but decisively, to say he had decided to give up his monthly talk. The decision was taken, virtually without discussion, not to attempt to replace him. To find another book-reviewer would have been simple; to replace E. M. Forster as a broadcaster to India was impossible.

His attitude to broadcasting in general was idealistic. He belonged to the generation to which "the wireless" came as a new and exciting dimension of experience, and to the section of that generation which clearly perceived the potentialities and responsibilities of the medium. As early as 1931 he wrote a letter to *The Spectator*, after the resignation of the then Director of Talks, Hilda Matheson, asserting that the B.B.C. had become too cautious and ending: "A timid B.B.C. is an appalling prospect, because, though timid, it will always be influential, and it will confirm thousands in our congenital habit of avoiding unwelcome truth."

He listened to "the wireless" from its early days, selectively and critically, often with pleasure, sometimes with excitement. He has continued to listen, with undiminished receptiveness, until (to my knowledge) quite recent years. As recently as 1958 he was one of the signatories—who included T. S. Eliot, Professor A. J. Ayer, Sir Adrian Boult, Earl Russell, Sir Arthur Bliss, and Sir John Gielgud—of a letter to *The Times* complaining about a change in the policy of the B.B.C. "in the direction of effortless listening which indicates a complete willingness to give up the struggle of requiring audiences to make an effort". In his own broadcasts he made the fullest effort to meet his audience; but he demanded of them the effort of following—as distinct from the half-attention of "drip-listening". Forster's reputation will endure in his novels, short stories, and criticism; but anyone who cares to study his broadcasts[1] will find in them a high technical standard and much of his character.

[1] Examples may be found in *Two Cheers for Democracy*, pp. 43–58, 62–71, 105–9, 136–9, 162–5, 174–7, 202–6, 229–36, 238–41, 246–50, 277–9, 296–8, 309–12, 327–35, 339–43 and 352–5; and in *The Listener* between 1930 and 1959.

Forster and his Publishers

by B. W Fagan

When Forster brought us the manuscript of his fifth novel, *A Passage to India*, in 1924, I was already a junior partner in the firm of Edward Arnold & Co., but was engaged on the educational side of the business and therefore had no hand in seeing the book through the press—a job which was naturally done by Arnold himself. (Incidentally, it is strange to remember that when Arnold first set eyes on the title he was disappointed and told me that he doubted whether it would sell well, on the ground that India was not at that time a popular subject with the general public. It may be partly for that reason that its first edition became one of the ugliest pieces of book production that have ever embodied a highly successful novel.)

In 1930, when Arnold retired from business, his work fell to me, and for thirty years, till my own retirement, I had the privilege of handling all Forster's books and came to know him well. But not too well too quickly: I was not very old, and not too sure of my competence for the job of dealing with such a high-powered author. I have never been entirely at ease in the company of literary persons, and I suspect that in those days something of the same sort of shyness may have affected him. Could it be that he was as much afraid of me as I was of him? Hardly, but I soon came to realise that never was a mind more acute allied with a spirit more modest, more natural, more unassuming, more unpompous. These characteristics are reflected, too, in his style of writing—the short words and simple sentences which beguile us by making difficult ideas seem easy.

It is these qualities that explain why someone so self-effacing became so successful as a broadcaster. The medium of sound reveals (as I believe television does not) the real personality of the speaker, and dispels mercilessly the fog of studied mannerisms by which some people attempt to create an image.

At the same time he has always been one to hold views firmly, to express them forcibly, and to make prompt decisions. In the middle 'thirties Allen Lane, when he was planning his Penguin series, came to see me about including a Forster novel (*Howards End*, I think) in his first batch. I duly put this proposal to Forster, who reflected for a little and then said: "Yes, I should like to be published at sixpence." And so it was. I also remember without pride that in reporting this to Lane I added that I gave his project a life of ten years, because by that time he would have exhausted the supply of best-selling novels. He was not impressed; he knew a better one than that.

In those days Forster and I were thrown together frequently. He has not in my time used a literary agent, and we discussed directly the terms of our publishing agreements (upon which no differences ever arose) as well as many points in his manuscripts themselves, upon which he was always ready to consider comments, and sometimes invited them. (One of these invitations led to trouble, as will appear later.)

The fact that he did not use an agent meant that many inquiries that would otherwise have gone there found their way to the publisher. It sometimes became a choice between worrying the author with petty requests and assuming on his behalf authority to which one had no right, as when the B.B.C. might ring up at the last moment asking leave for a quotation which it was strictly not our business to grant.

But in course of time I came to learn his mind on such matters, and it was possible to save him some trouble without making many mistakes. One incident gave me some malicious pleasure. One day I was rung up by a rasping and very businesslike American voice which wanted to be put in touch with Forster about the film rights of one of the novels. Film rights were not my affair, but I happened to know Forster's views on this subject. And so after stonewalling for some time I was delighted to hear the voice say "Don't you *want* to do business?" and to answer "No, I don't", which ended the conversation.

I think that Forster, in my early days at any rate, more than most authors shunned publicity, and we felt that we must be careful not to offend him by any extravagant expressions. It was some years before our advertising department could persuade me to persuade him to allow himself to be photographed for the purpose, and the comedy of errors that ensued on my first abortive attempt to bring the unwilling horse to the water is not suitable for performance here. But today nobody can stand against the pressure of the press, and I think that Forster, too, has to some extent overcome his reluctance to being discussed by all and sundry.

His occasional visits, whether with or without appointment, were characteristically free of formality. One of them remains in my mind, when he had called in to deliver a manuscript on his way to a short stay at his London retreat. Enter the author, carrying a battered and disreputable handbag—probably the article once described by William Plomer as "the sort of little bag that might have been carried in 1890 by the man who came to wind the clocks".[1] He plumps it down on my desk and, rummaging in it, takes out in succession a hairbrush, a newspaper, half a pair of pyjamas, two eggs in a brown paper bag ("Careful of these! They're my breakfasts"), a house-shoe, a book by Henry James, and various assorted articles. Finally from the bottom of the bag emerges the precious manuscript, it also a little wrinkled, but in perfect condition for use, and probably accompanied by a sheet of paper listing some passages on which he invites an opinion.

[1] *At Home* (Cape, London, 1958), p. 107.

One such invitation nearly led to disaster, as I mentioned earlier, and it may be of interest to recall this episode which led to an action for libel against the author and my firm. Neither of us had thought of himself as a libellous person, and this made it easier for us to be caught off our guard and trapped in a hidden noose.

In 1936 he made a selection of his occasional papers—essays, reviews, broadcast talks—to be issued as a volume under the title *Abinger Harvest*. With it he sent me a few others to look through in case any might strike me as worth adding. One in particular seemed so brilliant and amusing that I asked him to put it in, and he consented to do so. In due course the collection was published and so the train was laid. The explosion occurred a few days after publication and took the form of letters to publisher and author from a firm of solicitors on behalf of Sir Murdoch MacDonald, M.P., demanding withdrawal of the book and damages for libel in respect of the very article which I had persuaded Forster to include in it. This shock could not have come at a worse moment, for Forster was convalescent after an operation and in no condition to be worried with an affair of this kind. I drove down to Heytesbury, where he was staying with Siegfried Sassoon, and we agreed that I should get my firm's solicitors to defend the case on behalf of both of us and try to keep him out of it as far as possible. We had, of course, recalled all possible copies of the book and stopped the sale. When the solicitors got to work we had a further shock: they advised us that the libel was unquestionable, there was no defence, and the only course was to settle on the best terms possible. This was duly done on the basis of an apology in court, agreed damages for charity, and costs, the article to be excised before the book was reissued.

What was this devastating article which we had so foolishly and so innocently reprinted? It was four pages long, was entitled "A Flood in the Office", and consisted of a review, contributed to *The Athenaeum* in 1919, of a pamphlet entitled *The Nile Projects*, written by Sir William Willcocks and published in Egypt in the same year. I have never seen the pamphlet itself, but it must have been inflammatory. To judge by what the reviewer wrote, it recorded an "awful row" between two eminent engineers, expert on irrigation and water conservation, Sir William Willcocks and Sir Murdoch MacDonald, who had been advising the Egyptian Government about the treatment to be given to the River Nile. Their opinions had evidently differed profoundly, and Sir William's wrath had boiled over into this pamphlet, in which he accused Sir Murdoch of having falsified statistics, suborned witnesses at an inquiry, and committed other unethical practices. The review, amusing and light-hearted, took the line that the rights and wrongs of the controversy must be left to the technicians to decide, but that the pamphlet had painted for the ordinary man a vivid picture of old Father Nile.

Our solicitors in 1936 discovered that soon after publication of the pamphlet in 1919 Sir William had been prosecuted for criminal libel in the Egyptian courts, convicted, and bound over to keep the peace—an event of which neither Forster nor I had, of course, ever heard. But unfortunately his review quoted some of Sir William's statements, and our reprint had therefore repeated the libel that had already been condemned some seventeen years before, and probably been forgotten by everyone else.

It is easy to be wise now; and many may ask: "How could that hazard possibly have escaped you?" But perhaps one may be partly excused for having fallen into a trap that events had so cunningly set for us. Sir Murdoch behaved with propriety and without rancour, though he must have been furious, both personally and professionally, at the resurrection of the ghost he had thought to have laid for ever.

The tale has a happy ending: after the case was over, we were able to reissue *Abinger Harvest* without the offending passage, it started again on a long and successful life, and I was forgiven.

Apart from that one squall the course of relations between an author and his publisher can never have flowed more placidly than it has here; and there is no story in that.

But I have always been sorry that the public should have been

Forster as a Friend

by William Plomer

When I returned to England in 1929 many kindnesses were done to me by Leonard and Virginia Woolf, and it was they who introduced me to Morgan Forster. I was then twenty-five, and until this moment, when I have been doing a little mental arithmetic, it has never occurred to me that Morgan was then twice my age—a lead he has not managed to maintain.

He was a celebrity, though not in any popular sense, and I had little to my name except a novel and some short stories which had attracted some attention, and a youthful liveliness. One of the things I did have in common with him was a little unusual: each of us had lived in more than one country outside Europe and had become emotionally involved in it. (I think especially of Egypt in his case, and of Japan in mine.)

Because of long absence from this country when growing up I was a socially displaced person; I had no money and not much education; but such were the good graces of those elders and betters that they never said or did anything to remind me of my shortcomings. They made me feel accepted and anxious to please; they had no doubt noticed that, like them, I was not one who invariably took conventional belief and behaviour for granted.

I remember Morgan's very first invitation to me: he asked me to lunch at the Reform Club. Perhaps thinking his guest shy, he came hospitably to the entrance to meet me, and at once put the Reform's sombre and stately atrium in perspective by glancing at his fingers and saying quizzically: "I do find, don't you, that housework is *so* bad for the hands."

A young writer living precariously in some hired room, and with no money-making propensity, was naturally grateful for hospitality which provided him with the attention of a distinguished man, entrancing conversations, and proper meals. Morgan went further. From the time I first knew him he always had a flat in London, in Brunswick Square for some years and later overlooking Turnham Green, and in the days when I had no roof I could call my own he was good enough to lend me his flat from time to time when he was absent, and so give me, in his generous and imaginative way, a temporary privacy and independence.

In those days he was not based at King's, as in later years after the death of his mother, but at West Hackhurst, the house at Abinger Hammer where he and she were established. I have written in my book, *At Home*, some impressions of visits to West Hackhurst and do not wish to repeat them here, except to recall that as late as the end of the Second World War the atmosphere was delightfully reminiscent of the early Edwardian world of his novels. The house and its furniture seemed almost wholly pre-1900. Agnes, the elderly house-parlourmaid, and Bone, the elderly gardener, were nineteenth-century characters both in dress and manners; and the style and tempo of everyday life, down to the patterned jug and basin on the washstand in one's bedroom, were the same as in houses I had known during my Edwardian childhood.

It was curiously comforting and restful to escape to West Hackhurst from London and motor traffic and Great Wars and emotional wear-and-tear and the business of earning one's living, and a pleasure to know Mrs. Forster and to see the mutual affection between mother and son. I can remember him doing things to please her which he can hardly have wanted to do, and doing them with a good grace. And I am reminded of other instances of his extraordinary patience in attending to the concerns of persons he was fond of. Here is one. He had generously agreed to act as an executor for a friend's relation, a woman whom he hardly knew and who had not long to live. He could hardly have foreseen that this would involve him, for several years and more than other responsibilities of the kind, in a dreadfully boring periodic routine of signing and posting batches of papers having to do with a shoal of small investments held in trust. Though he might reasonably have felt that his kindness had been taken advantage of, not a word of complaint from him was ever heard or heard of.

As soon as I got to know Morgan it was easy to see how much his friends meant to him. I noticed that he never used expressions like "a friend of mine", or "a woman I know", or "as somebody said the other day", or "some people I was staying with". Everybody was alluded to by name, with a curious kind of emphasis or relish. This did not mean that he was like Hugh Walpole, who used to draw up at the end of every year a list of his forty-five best friends, divided into first class and second class, a list annually subject to drastic revision: the elect were liable, if any had given offence by what they had done or *not* done, to be dropped like hot potatoes. But Morgan's habit did, at first, remind me a little of some women who, apparently feeling a need to sustain their own identities, allude by name to friends whom they regard as smart, grand, charming or clever. "I've just come back," a woman of this kind may say, "from a wonderful week with the Elvaston-Clunches," regardless that one has never heard of them and is without a clue to the nature of their wonder-working.

With Morgan things were quite different. His allusions to persons I had never met or even heard of did make them seem, because of their special importance to him and consequent graduation into his private élite, rather larger than life-size. But I noticed that when persons were named any quoted remark was joyfully attributed to its maker. And it seemed perfectly right for a novelist to regard living persons as characters—almost, one felt, as "his" characters—and to delight, as Forster has always done, in their characteristic sayings. He showed himself to be quite unlike worldly persons who are cautious and reserved about naming their intimates, and also completely unlike those emotionally insecure or reserved or suspicious persons who secretively keep their friends apart. Clearly he was a novelist peopling his life, as it were, with characters, and himself living, as in a novel, in a network of relationships with them.

On some occasion of our meeting, thirty years or more ago, he might remark: "I've just been seeing Florence Barger." One felt that this was a momentous occurrence, but when he didn't at all explain who Mrs. Barger was, or why he had been seeing her, or the consequences, it did not seem polite to press for enlightenment. I did instantly understand that he was fond of her, that she was important to him, seemed to him unique, and must surely be, for that very reason, in some way exceptional. I also understood that it was not *his* identity that Morgan was sustaining, but *hers*— though I must say Mrs. Barger (like some other persons alluded to *passim*, English perhaps, or Indian, or American) never quite swam into focus for me. I never saw her—or, if I did, I don't remember her. She is to me like one of many names (some belonging to persons well known to me) in an imaginary list of "characters in the order of their appearance", with Rosalie, Malcolm Darling, darling May, Masood, Charles Mauron, Bill Roerick, Cousin Horace, and all. In that list of characters in the living novel of Morgan's life I could suppose her to be entered as "Mrs. Florence Barger, a wise and sympathetic confidante".

Morgan has always been completely unlike those who pursue or frequent or bandy about the names of the famous in order to seem famous themselves. In fact, he has been such a rare specialist in detecting and bringing out the qualities of "ordinary" persons, and in making them feel they mattered to him, that I believe not one of his closest intimates has ever been eminent in a worldly sense. Every one of them was found by him to be in some way at least un-ordinary, and it could be part of a biographer's business to discover in what ways he found them so. I think it might appear that Morgan was sometimes as instantly drawn to some of those he got to know and like best by some chance remark, some overlooked utterance in print, some quirk of behaviour, as by physical allure.

When Morgan was in Egypt there were many Englishmen there, but it was he who "discovered" Cavafy as a man and first made him known to the English-speaking world as a poet. To say that Morgan's friendship has often been creative means not only that he has recognised and stimulated the individuality of persons he has been fond of but that in some instances he has put them in the way of literary creativeness. I am thinking in particular of Joe Ackerley and his *Hindoo Holiday*. It is not difficult to see an affinity between Ackerley's candour and directness and Morgan's own ability to take short cuts to truth through formal thickets of accepted ideas, though these two did not always go in the same direction: animals and birds, for example, have never been given by Morgan the precedence given to them by Ackerley, who took to advocating zoolatry, not humanism.

An important function in Morgan's friendships has been his letter-writing. He was, when one comes to think of it, born a mid-Victorian, and so grew up to manhood in a world without telephones. He must have written a great many letters in his time, and a great many of them must have dealt with matters now usually dealt with by telephone—appointments, invitations and such things—but no doubt a great proportion have been communications with friends on less routine subjects. If a quantity of his letters to his friends is ever printed, they may be found to be no more like anybody else's letters than he is like anybody else. It is a safe guess that they will show affection and constancy; patience with the tiresomeness of others, as well as sudden and even sharp impatience when tiresomeness seemed to have gone too far; the same tendency to moralise and even dogmatise which is found in his printed writings, and the same sort of wisdom; a conspicuous absence of pomposity and self-importance, but occasional indications that it must not be presumed upon; repeated darts of direct comment which not only go straight to a variety of points but through them to whatever is hidden beyond; and—except when he was displeased with his correspondent—that special characteristic of his, a lambent playfulness.

It is a rare sort of feat to have won the confidence and affection of that assortment of persons whose names make up the list I have imagined of dramatis personae. Let us pretend that Morgan's greatest novel is his life. It may have fictive elements (whose life hasn't?), but is stranger than fiction. In it come and go (or come and stay) persons of widely differing racial origins, religious backgrounds, social habits and class-consciousness, some of the highest literacy, some of none at all, some with plenty of money, some without expectations. One might wonder whether some of them have had much in common beyond being bipeds with the faculty of engaging and responding to his affection.

At this point it seems fitting to recall that credo of his, *What I Believe* (1939), which is included in *Two Cheers for Democracy* (1951). In it he declared his belief in what he called "an aristocracy of the sensitive, the considerate and the plucky". I think we can assume that he would regard his tried friends as belonging to this élite. He went on to explain that these aristocrats "are sensitive for others as well as for themselves . . . considerate without being fussy", and that by pluck he means "the power to endure" (TC, 82–3).

It does rather seem that it might be all too possible for one of them to lose caste by some deficiency in sensitiveness or by some excess of considerateness. I cannot help saying that the word "plucky", though it has an ancient derivation, seems obsolescent and for me has an unpleasant "period" association. It immediately recalls the too self-confident young wife of an Edwardian schoolmaster, of the "muscular Christian" type, advertising her approval of virility in the male young. Trying to set aside this distaste for the word—a distaste I regret, because the definition of Morgan's aristocracy makes it seem so attractive—I feel uncertain about "the power to endure". To endure *what*? I ask. And what about the power to refuse to endure, the power to *resist*?

The same paper contains an often-quoted declaration which must be considered by anybody who wants to try to understand Morgan's conception and technique (if I may use the word) of friendship. "If I had to choose," he wrote, "between betraying my country and betraying my friend, I hope I should have the guts to betray my country." This is, I think, a more difficult saying than it looks. Certainly Brutus and Cassius chose "to betray their friend Julius Caesar rather than their country Rome" (T C, 78). But the issue might not be so simple. One can imagine a situation in which "love and loyalty to an individual" might involve the betrayal of a number of other no less loved individuals whose existence was inseparable from the safety, defence and hopes of one's country.

One of Morgan's greatest virtues is his lifelong struggle to get at and formulate exact truths and the relations between different truths, and so to do away with "muddle" (one of his favourite words). If one cannot invariably concur with the result, that does nothing to lessen admiration for what he has done or tried to do. If ever it becomes possible to take a full view of his life and character as well as of his writings, it may be recognised that one of his most creative achievements has been his avoidance of muddle in making friends—a conclusion with which, I hope, those of them who survive might all join in agreement.

Forster on Love and
Money

by Wilfred Stone

In 1957 Forster said to Angus Wilson: "Yes. Butler influenced me, of course. He taught me how to look at money when I was young."[1] It is a surprising statement, even at first sight a little shocking, and strangers to Forster might well wonder whether Butler is being pulled up or down a peg. For the subject of money can still seem a strangely illicit or disquieting presence in polite company, something that should be mentioned, if at all, furtively, apologetically, or with professional seriousness. Quaint though it seems today to hear that Edith Wharton as a girl was advised never to "talk about money and [to] think about it as little as possible",[2] and that Forster as a boy was told "Dear, don't talk about money, it's ugly" (TC, 68), we still have no difficulty in understanding that Victorian reticence. As Butler said, "next to sexual matters there are none upon which there is such complete reserve between parents and children as on those connected with money."[3] There are, indeed, intimate connections between sex

---

[1] "A Conversation with E. M. Forster", *Encounter*, IX (Nov. 1957), 55.
[2] Alfred Kazin, *On Native Grounds* (abridged ed., Doubleday, New York, 1956), p. 74.
[3] Quoted from *The Notebooks of Samuel Butler*, ed. H. F. Jones, by P. N. Furbank, *Samuel Butler (1835–1902)* (Cambridge University Press, 1948), p. 20.

and money,[4] and we may have become more emancipated regarding the former than the latter. Certain it is that lucre, in at least some of its aspects, can still seem "filthy", and for many people can be decently invoked only after the proper ritual preparation.

Forster broke through these inhibitions again and again—deliberately and with calculated effect. When he has Margaret Schlegel of *Howards End* shout "Hurrah for riches!" or "Money for ever!" (p. 65) he is being deliberately outrageous, openly defying that prudery about money that his generation had confused with good taste. As Margaret develops her theme, she goes straight to the heart of a major Victorian and Edwardian hypocrisy:

> "I'm tired of these rich people who pretend to be poor, and think it shows a nice mind to ignore the piles of money that keep their feet above the waves. I stand each year upon six hundred pounds, and Helen upon the same, and Tibby will stand upon eight, and as fast as our pounds crumble away into the sea they are renewed—from the sea, yes, from the sea. And all our thoughts are the thoughts of six-hundred-pounders, and all our speeches. . . ." (p. 64.)

Forster is here, to use his own language, being "coarse"—coarse on his own principle that distinguishes coarseness as "revealing something" from vulgarity as "concealing something" (LJ, 234). The principle is fundamental in Forster's scheme of value, and can be seen as the divide separating the saved from the damned (which is almost to say the pagans from the puritans) in all his work. The Schlegel sisters were, he writes, tactless and "heavy-handed" about money: they "held that reticence about money matters is absurd, and that life would be truer if each would state the exact size of the golden island upon which he stands, the

---

[4] Freud repeatedly illustrates the unconscious connections in human fantasy life between money and sexuality, particularly between money and various aspects of anal eroticism. In *Anxiety and Instinctual Life* he writes: "Faeces—money—gift—baby—penis are treated as though they meant the same thing, and they are represented too by the same symbols." *The Standard Edition of the Complete Psychological Works of Sigmund Freud*, ed. James Strachey, vol. 22 (Hogarth Press and Institute of Psycho-Analysis, London, 1966), p. 101.

exact stretch of warp over which he throws the woof that is not money" (HE, 149). But Sawston, that hateful philistine suburb which symbolises everything Forster rejects in his own class, regards such self-exposure as obscene. Sawston is vulgar—tight, withdrawn, secretive, purse-proud, class-proud—and Henry Wilcox, its chief representative in *Howards End*, "winced a little" at the mention of the word "money", and was unable to reveal even to his future wife how much he was worth (HE, 190). Sawston is, as Freud would say, anal, and in its anality Forster saw something corrupt and evil. It is the same corruption that John Maynard Keynes inveighed against in blasting Benthamism as "the worm which has been gnawing at the insides of modern civilisation and is responsible for its present moral decay"[5]— and in charting a course to prosperity and full employment via spending and consumption rather than via those prime virtues of the puritan code: thrift and abstinence. "When the accumulation of wealth is no longer of high social importance," writes Keynes, "there will be great changes in the code of morals. . . . The love of money as a possession—as distinguished from the love of money as a means to the enjoyments and realities of life—will be recognised for what it is, a somewhat disgusting morbidity, one of those semi-criminal, semi-pathological propensities which one hands over with a shudder to the specialists in mental disease."[6]

This emphasis is revolutionary, and Forster in sharing it had the insight to see that money is not only a commercial symbol, but a counter in the transactions of the spirit—in the whole moral and psychological drama of life. In a sense money is to Forster what sex is to Lawrence: a medium of exchange that can, in a particular transaction, symbolically reflect much beyond itself—the health of society or the course of history or the psychic bondage of individuals. When, for example, Miss Beaumont, in the story "Other Kingdom", flees for her life from the Midas-touch of her would-be lover, a rich Benthamite who looks on a wife as a possession, she cries: "Oh, fence me out if you like! Fence me out as

[5] *Two Memoirs* (Hart-Davis, London, 1949), p. 96.
[6] *Essays in Persuasion* (Macmillan, London, 1931), p. 369.

much as you like! But never in. Oh, Harcourt, never in. I must
be . . . where anyone can reach me." (css, 76.) This is a glimpse
of the fictional dialectic between vulgarity and coarseness that
goes on throughout Forster's work. Miss Beaumont's coarseness
saves her, her spiritual promiscuity is a new (almost Keynesian)
version of the old hedonistic argument that beauty's coin should
be current and not hoarded.[7]

The fact that money as such is not mentioned in the story makes
no difference: the metaphors of love and money are interchange-
able and inseparable. And just as love can be thought of as sacred
and profane (Agape and Eros), so money can have (at least) these
different roles. Money *connects* even as love does (when it is used as
a means of fulfilment), and when it is absent or misused it can have
the opposite effect, as Margaret so plainly saw: "Last night, when
we were talking up here round the fire, I began to think that the
very soul of the world is economic, and that the lowest abyss is
not the absence of love, but the absence of coin." (he, 64).
Forster does not, as Norman Kelvin maintains,[8] see money as
necessarily corrupting; it is simply a neutral counter in a game
between vulgarity and coarseness, a counter that can be good or
evil, creative or destructive, depending on the motives of those
who use it.

In this preoccupation with money Forster is not alone; the
theme runs throughout Victorian and Edwardian literature. The
filthy "dust-heaps" of Dickens's *Our Mutual Friend* anticipate
Margaret's "piles of money" by fifty years[9] and give Freudians
their great opportunity—but the theme appears in all the major
writers: Thackeray, James, Trollope, Conrad, Hardy, Shaw,
Wells, Lawrence. The reason is, of course, the Industrial Revolution and the impact of a money economy on a culture that had,
until shortly before, been agrarian and semi-feudal. But from

[7] See, for example, Milton's *Comus*, lines 739–40.
[8] *E. M. Forster* (Southern Illinois University Press, Carbondale,
Illinois, 1967), p. 28.
[9] Forster has the Wilcoxes sweep in and out of Oniton "leaving a little
dust and a little money behind" (he, 264).

about 1870 on, as England expanded her empire and overseas
markets, a rather special element entered the picture: the money
continued to pour in (for the upper middle classes), but increasingly from invisible sources, from manipulation rather than work,
from shares, or, as Margaret has it, "from the sea". The visible
connection between labour and reward, sowing and reaping, was
reduced, and a generation brought up on the Victorian work-ethic
had to face the moral crisis occasioned by receiving vast sums of
money they had neither earned nor felt they deserved. To the
puritan mind this is virtually synonymous with corruption, and
perhaps the rarest hero of Victorian literature is the character who,
though rich, stays honest, like Trollope's Palliser. But what is
most marked in this literature is the portrayal of rich people
rationalising their unconscious guilt, as James's Mrs. Gereth tries
to transmute the glut of her "things"—her accumulation of furniture—into what she calls "the beauty" or "the works of art".
Forster, too, appears to have felt this guilt, and in a particularly
personal way[10]—especially, it would seem, during those pre-war
years when he wrote *The Longest Journey* (1907), "Other Kingdom"
(1909), and *Howards End* (1910). Of this period George Orwell
wrote: "There never was, I suppose, in the history of the world a
time when the sheer vulgar fatness of wealth, without any kind of
aristocratic elegance to redeem it, was so obtrusive as in those
years before 1914."[11]

Forster felt this vulgarity, but he was conscious of living off
some of the fat, and this tension is deeply reflected in some of his
best work. There is little doubt about his ideal: it was expressed
in a fantasy about his own great-grandfather, who, Forster wrote,

[10] Although Forster was only eight when his paternal great-aunt left
him a legacy of £8,000, it seems likely that he had this legacy in mind
when he makes Ansell declare that Stephen Wonham "would sooner
die than take money from people he did not love" (LJ, 254); for, as
with great honesty he tells us, he "had not really loved Aunt Monie—
she was too old, and the masses of presents she had given me had not
found their way to my tiny heart". (MT, 287.)
[11] "Such, Such Were the Joys", *In Front of Your Nose (Collected Essays,
Journalism and Letters*, vol. 4; Secker & Warburg, London, and Harcourt, Brace, New York, 1968), p. 357.

lived in an age when "to get rich and to be good were harmonious" (TC, 199). Can a rich man enter the kingdom of heaven? Forster had moments when, pondering his own family history, he imagined this to be possible. But this ideal, however desirable for Forster's peace of mind, is only a momentary wish-fulfilment. More fundamental and permanent is the split in his allegiance between the two sides of his family: the father's side, descended from the Claphamite Thorntons, representing wealth, power, and sobriety; and the mother's side, the Whichelos, representing poverty, inefficiency, and love. It was this split that made the dream of harmony necessary—money and love, Caesar's coin as well as God's—for only through this dual possession could the terrible breach be healed, and guilt be expunged. Again and again this question is negotiated in his work; indeed, the joining of the seen and the unseen, the incarnation of the world and the spirit, is the motive behind all his art. "Will it really profit us so much if we save our souls and lose the whole world?" (LJ, 256) is a typical re-phrasing of a biblical injunction in order to meet this moral crisis, as also is Margaret Schlegel's reply to the question of "what it would profit Mr. Bast if he gained the whole world and lost his own soul". "Nothing, but he would not gain his soul until he had gained a little of the world." (HE, 135.) Yet another is the question he asks in *Howards End* about the house he has simultaneously treated as a piece of real estate and as a symbolic house representing something spiritual, the "best self" of England:

> To them Howards End was a house: they could not know that to her it had been a spirit, for which she sought a spiritual heir. And—pushing one step farther in these mists—may they not have decided even better than they supposed? Is it credible that the possessions of the spirit can be bequeathed at all? Has the soul offspring? (p. 104.)

But to return to an earlier consideration: what is it that Butler might have taught Forster about money?[12] First it is worth noting

[12] For more light on this see Lee Elbert Holt, "E. M. Forster and Samuel Butler", *PMLA*, LXI (Sept. 1946), 813–14.

that Butler was for at least ten years a strong influence on Forster. Forster read with excitement *The Way of All Flesh* when it appeared in 1903, a book that Mr. Beebe of *A Room With A View* (1908) had, the worse for him, "never heard of" (RV, 153). He drew Mr. Emerson of the same novel at least partially after Butler; he did an essay on his "hero" in 1910, and in 1914 had contracted to do a book on him when the war intervened. There is no immediate way of tracing precisely just where or how Butler's influence was exerted, but a critical statement by Daniel F. Howard in his Introduction to *The Way of All Flesh* gives us some good clues. He writes:

> Ernest recovers from his attempt to become a lower-class man and from his false marriage under the nursing of Overton, a rich, essentially classless man who comments on the world in stage burlesques—a bachelor who is fortunate enough to have seen the only woman he might have married die before the mistake was made. Overton's medicine for Ernest proves to be gold, a nostrum so dangerous as well as efficacious that he has had to withhold it until his patient's case is most critical. Then large doses cure Ernest, but with money he too can be classless—part of no profession or trade: not a clergyman or a tailor or a shopkeeper; not of the natural aristocracy of Towneley, the middle class of his family, or the lower class of Ellen. With money, Ernest finds himself in the same position of economic power as a long line of characters in the English novel, from Moll Flanders to Becky Sharp and Pip and Bulstrode; but unlike these characters he does not try to use his money to buy into the fashionable world, to establish himself within an already existing social structure. Money in this novel is not the means for realising social dreams—a plantation in Virginia, a fashionable life in London, a respected name in Middlemarch; rather it is an absolution from the necessity of seeking any place at all within society.[13]

If we replace Ernest's name here with that of Leonard Bast, and Overton's with that of Helen Schlegel, the similarity between Butler's theme and Forster's in *Howards End* is immediately apparent. The epigraph of Forster's book is, we remember, "Only

[13] Introduction to *Ernest Pontifex, or The Way of All Flesh* (Houghton Mifflin, Boston, 1964), p. xviii.

connect . . .", and one of the most important connections occurs between Helen Schlegel, one of Forster's "saved", and Leonard, a poor young man on the very bottom edge of the middle class. His class position is important, for, as Forster says, "We are not concerned with the very poor. They are unthinkable. . . . This story deals with gentlefolk, or with those who are obliged to pretend that they are gentlefolk." (HE, 47–8.) The only admissible class is the middle class, for it alone—here Forster is following Matthew Arnold—is capable of achieving what Arnold called "culture".

But what is important to see is that "culture" is a condition of classlessness, a peculiar state of grace—the state that the Schlegels are presumed to possess from the start and that Overton helps Ernest achieve by his gift of gold. Helen does precisely what Overton does—or tries to—by offering Leonard a gift outright of £5,000, an act that causes her brother Tibby to exclaim, in one of his rare outbursts of passion, "Good God alive!" (p. 269).[14] When Leonard refuses the money, Tibby is pleased, for "Bast seemed somewhat a monumental person after all" (p. 270). But Helen is "frantic", desperate with unappeased guilt, for to her Leonard's act indicates his unwillingness to be "saved". Why? Because the money was his ticket to classlessness, to that condition, as Arnold would say, beyond his classbound "ordinary self" (by which we are "separate, personal, at war"), to his classless "best self" (by which we are "united, impersonal, at harmony").[15] Tibby, whose sense of value is at the very least undependable, sees only the monumental self-denial of the act, which he obviously does not expect from one of Leonard's station. But Helen is looking beyond class to that state of transcendence where all the barriers are down. Leonard's refusal means that he is still obeying the *mores* of class instead of his own inner promptings. One of the tenets of the middle class is that gifts of money are given only to servants,

[14] Rickie Elliot also commits the "unpardonable sin" (LJ, 58) of offering a hundred pounds a year to some people who need it.
[15] "Doing As One Likes", *The Portable Matthew Arnold*, ed. Lionel Trilling (Viking, New York, 1949), pp. 523–4.

while gifts of objects are given to equals;[16] so to the still class-bound Leonard the offer can only appear humiliating. He is still too "vulgar", his heart is still too "full of little things" (p. 252) to drop his defences and trust himself to the open spaces of freedom afforded by Helen's money. Helen's earlier aim had been "to cut the rope that fastened Leonard to the earth" (p. 253), to get him to value the claims of the Invisible as against the Visible—the claims of music, of poetry, of nature, of all-night walks through the Surrey countryside, of love, and even of death. But Leonard, having lost his job and income through her good offices, is disillusioned and returns to the safety of his class prejudices. "The real thing's money," he says, "and all the rest is a dream." Against this cynicism Helen argues furiously that a thing more real is Death: "I love Death—not morbidly, but because He explains. He shows me the emptiness of Money. Death and Money are the eternal foes. Not Death and Life." (p. 252.)

How can one who a few pages later tries to give away £5,000 make this speech? She can make it because £5,000 is not "Money" but "Fortune". The dispensing of largesse on this scale partakes of the nature of a divine gift; it is like those other large abstractions that Helen uses to seduce Leonard away from his vulgar commitment to class values: "Behind the coffins and the skeletons that stay the vulgar mind lies something so immense that all that is great in us responds to it." (p. 253.) Helen's fantastic bribe partakes of that immensity, and tries to lure Leonard into it; but he has already suffered too much at the hands of outrageous fortune to risk any more.

That Helen here, in trying to buy a man's soul, may be playing the Devil's part is a possibility that neither she nor her author seems to consider very seriously.[17] Though Helen is far from

16 " 'We always give the servants money.' 'Yes, do you, yes, much easier,' replied Margaret, but felt the grotesque impact of the unseen upon the seen, and saw issuing from a forgotten manger at Bethlehem this torrent of coins and toys. Vulgarity reigned." (HE, 85.)
17 In *Where Angels Fear to Tread* an Englishwoman tries to buy an Italian baby, and in "The Eternal Moment" another Englishwoman asks for one—and apparently expects to get it.

perfect (she is shown to be hysterical, frigid, even a little cruel), she is nevertheless placed among the saved; her motives and money are seen to be pure—or at least purifying—and she, in spite of her faults, helps to demonstrate the possibility of that ideal world where to be rich and to be good can be harmonious. But the reader is troubled by the demonstration, troubled mainly by the fact that she seems to save herself at the expense of Leonard, and be blessed for it. For example, after having loved Leonard absolutely "perhaps for half an hour" (p. 335), she then rejects him: "I want never to see him again, though it sounds appalling. I wanted to give him money and feel finished." (p. 330.) Clearly the money is her substitute for love and her payment for absolution—absolution from that guilt which Erich Fromm has seen as original, the guilt of separation. Had Leonard taken the money, we are led to believe, all would have been well; he would have been saved and Helen's moral quit-claim would have been honoured. As it is her conscience is appeased only as she "forgets" Leonard, and as he slips into degradation:

> It is true that Helen offered him five thousand pounds, but such a sum meant nothing to him. He could not see that the girl was desperately righting herself, and trying to save something out of the disaster, if it was only five thousand pounds. But he had to live somehow. He turned to his family, and degraded himself to a professional beggar. There was nothing else for him to do. (p. 335.)

He has slipped not into the classlessness of the Butlerian or Arnoldian sort—uncommitted to any profession or trade—but into a lower form of the same thing: unemployability.

Yet at the end of the book Helen is shown with her child and beloved sister in a kind of garden of innocence at Howards End, and Leonard is dead—dead, we might say, as a direct consequence of his fatal refusal to take the money and its spiritual rewards. He has been a living proof of Margaret's earlier claim that a man of his class "might be given anything and everything so long as it was not the money itself" (p. 133). It is a strange kind of poetic justice, and we begin to understand it only when we recognise that this book is partly a kind of romance-allegory and partly a realistic novel. In trying to demonstrate how the coinage of earth and that of heaven might be connected, Forster effects certain symbolic exchanges, transmutations, so to speak, of base materials into gold. One of these is the transformation of "squalor" into "tragedy". In the value terms of the book, squalor is bad and tragedy is good; squalor breeds vulgarity, tragedy coarseness; the one is retentive and class-bound, the other transcends these confines to openness, prodigality, heroism—to a condition that doesn't count the *cost*. Early in the book, speaking of Leonard and his Jacky, the narrator says: "His had scarcely been a tragic marriage. Where there is no money and no inclination to violence tragedy cannot be generated." (p. 130.) Yet sometimes squalor can be associated with greatness (which was what Helen hoped for Leonard): "Squalor and tragedy can beckon to all that is great in us, and strengthen the wings of love. They can beckon; it is not certain that they will, for they are not love's servants." (p. 342.) But at the close, as Leonard lies dead, the narrator says: "Let Squalor be turned into Tragedy, whose eyes are the stars, and whose hands hold the sunset and the dawn." (p. 349.) This is a fulfilment of Helen's earlier dictum: "Death destroys a man: the idea of Death saves him" (p. 253), for tragedy is the "idea" of death—not mere physical dying but physical dying translated into "greatness" or "heroism"—and Leonard's end is seen as tragic.

Thus is the base metal transmuted. It is a beautiful symbolism, and intriguing as well as beautiful. The only trouble is that the "tragedy" seems to be performed almost solely for the benefit of the Schlegels. The close of the book shows all the leading males either dead, exhausted, or imprisoned, while Helen and Margaret settle peacefully into Howards End, inheritors of both the material and the spiritual house. As the symphonic close of a kind of allegorical romance, this is moving; but as the resolution of a realistic problem in human relationships it is decidedly unfair. Much depends on whether we read this book as romance or realism, as a myth in which all the people and events are symbolic parts of an aesthetic design, or as a novel in which the people and events have a realistic social, psychological, and moral existence.

It is next to impossible not to read it both ways, but to the very end the romance will not mix with the realism—a fact which in itself suggests the impossibility, or at least intractability, of the problem Forster set for himself: the connecting of earthly and spiritual treasure. For if we refuse to be beguiled by the allegorical design, we find it hard to accept the Schlegels—who are, after all, people and not goddesses—as such unquestioned arbiters of value. Was not Leonard *right* to distrust Helen and her missionary impulses? Given the mistiness of her value-world, should we not be more encouraged to honour his refusal to be declassed? Is she really in command of her own motives? The unbeguiled reader could be excused if he read mainly hostility and devilment in that offer of cold cash. Gold since ancient times has been known, in one of its manifestations, as the Devil's dung, and Leonard had reason to feel that the offer of £5,000 was as much flung at him as given. But of course the true answer is that money is dual: it is both holy and profane, sacred and secular; it is the stuff both of heaven and of hell—and thus it is a useful agent in effecting a marriage between the two. That marriage in *Howards End* is not quite made, but Forster has given us an unforgettable look at the way money—that peculiarly modern symbol of value—can serve as the medium of exchange.

"Pecunia non olet," Vespasian is supposed to have said in defending a tax on urinals, money doesn't stink.[18] This is as true as the opposite insight: that lucre is "filthy". Where money is the theme, olfactory metaphors are frequently found, and they occur with fair abundance in *Howards End*. Most conspicuously, whenever Margaret meets Jacky her nostrils are assaulted by "odours from the abyss" (p. 124): "Mrs. Lanoline had risen out of the

[18] The story is told by Suetonius in *The Lives of the Twelve Caesars*, trans. Alexander Thomson, Book 10 (Bell, London, 1911), p. 460; but the phrase is a medieval invention. See also Bernard W. Henderson, *Five Roman Emperors* (Cambridge University Press, 1927), p. 6.

abyss, like a faint smell, a goblin footfall, telling of a life where love and hatred had both decayed." (p. 121.) Love and hatred have both decayed, and why? Not, of course, because of the presence of money—though money can have this effect, as Lawrence's "The Rocking-Horse Winner" attests—but because there is so little of it, because the straitened circumstances of their lives allow no escape from a niggling preoccupation with petty cash and petty property and the petty values that go with them. As Margaret says: "A big windfall would not pauperise a man. It is these little driblets, distributed among too many, that do the harm." (p. 134.)

The lower world smells because it is close and narrow, because its squalor is suffocating, because it is vulgar—tight, defensive, cautious, penny-pinching, thrifty, suspicious. Its evils are like the evils of "reticence", which Forster repeatedly invokes: "His reticence was not entirely the shoddy article that a business life promotes, the reticence that pretends that nothing is something, and hides behind the *Daily Telegraph*." (p. 131.) The antidote to this world is the world of nature and of space, the "eternity of beauty" surrounding Howards End, the sweet smell of hay and flowers. The journey from the abyss to classlessness is a passage from an evil-smelling place into "sweetness and light". Money, when used to pay for that passage, is a holy thing, but money as the Wilcoxes know and use it is the opposite; their motor-cars are always "stinking". "They had no part with the earth and its emotions. They were dust, and a stink, and cosmopolitan chatter." (p. 226.) When Margaret marries Henry her narrator writes: "She, a monogamist, regretted the cessation of some of life's innocent odours . . ." (p. 272); and one can say that her marriage was one long attempt to deodorise it. The issue, then, is not just money or its absence, but certain psychological and moral attitudes that money can evoke or demonstrate. The best condition is a kind of spiritual prodigality that does no book-keeping. Margaret is for "generosity" over "justice"—"Be generous to them. . . . Bother justice!" (p. 190)—for aristocratic openhandedness over the nice parcelling out of fair shares. And we know Leonard has good in him when he ponders the fate of Jacky in these words: "Would she ever receive the justice that is mercy—the justice for by-products that the world is too busy to bestow?" (p. 336.) Mercy is to justice as infinity is to the abyss, as tragedy is to squalor, as generosity is to anality, as the smell of hay is to the stink of a motor-car.

These exchanges have many variants, but money is the symbolic medium of exchange. As the Schlegels look back on the action of the book, they congratulate themselves that the inner life has "paid". The commercial vocabulary persists even in the realm of the spirit, just as Forster's Clapham ancestors used the language of the market-place in religious matters, so that the soul "closed with the offer of God in Christ" or "acquired a saving interest in the Blood of Jesus"[19] (TC, 200). Likewise *Howards End* can be looked upon as one big "deal", in which Schlegel negotiations reward them (in spite of and almost because of their unbusiness-like prodigalities) with a vast increase of treasure both upon earth and in heaven. The trouble with his Clapham ancestors, Forster said, was that they never felt the need of being lifted into "a region outside money" (TC, 200). *Howards End* shows not only a fantasy of how that might be done, but shows as well that there might be money in it.

What must one do to be saved? Sell all that thou hast and give to the poor? No. Forster, remembering Tolstoy, would have none of that; yet all his life he was torn between forces of retentiveness and forces of openhandedness. The scene in the "Dell" in *The Longest Journey* is central. There Rickie is shown as desiring "to love every one equally" (LJ, 27)—which is another way of desiring to share universally one's wealth—but this lovely feeling turns out to be possible only with a small and select group of friends, and even they see the desire as promiscuous and wrong. Nevertheless, to share this way is to get rid of guilt, for it is a total denial of one's "vulgarity" and an absolute expression of one's love.

Those tragi-comic missionaries of *A Passage to India*, old Mr. Graysford and young Mr. Sorley, conclude their discussion about who shall be admitted into heaven by saying: "We must exclude someone from our gathering, or we shall be left with nothing." (PI, 41.) Money to be sanctified must be used in the way of love, as Zeus impregnated Danae in a shower of gold (semen), but at last even love in Forster's view must be curtailed. "Love is a great force in private life . . . but love in public affairs does not work." (TC, 56.) Forster's problem remains: how to find a division that "will render unto the community what is the community's, and to the self what is the self's. We have not found it, and the New Jerusalem cannot be built until we do.[20] The statement is a paraphrase of the biblical injunction "Render to Caesar the things that are Caesar's, and to God the things that are God's" (Mark 12:17), and represents both a major preoccupation of Forster and the problem he never solved. But it is part of Forster's distinction that he saw the importance of a problem, kept his conscience alive to it, and opened our eyes to the possibility that money may have become our most viable modern symbol—and the medium for purchasing God's things as well as Caesar's. It is his distinction, too, that he came out on the side of generosity, openness and spending (with their sexual and moral as well as economic implications), in defiance, or at least partial defiance, of that tight Victorian world in which he was nurtured. This partisanship has helped to define his spirit, and to make it still revolutionary and life-giving.

[20] "The Ivory Tower", *London Mercury*, XXIX (Dec. 1938), 126.

Two Passages to India: Forster as Victorian and Modern

by Malcolm Bradbury

There are major writers whose work seems to us important as a contribution to the distinctive powers and dimensions of art; there are others whose work represents almost a personal appeal to value, and who therefore live—for certain of their readers, at least—with a singular force. There have not been many English novelists of our own time who have established with us the second function, but E. M. Forster is certainly one of them. He has served as an embodiment of the virtues he writes about; he has shown us their function and their destiny; he has left, for other writers and other men, a workable inheritance. Partly this is because he has always regarded art as a matter of intelligence as well as passion, honesty as well as imagination. In making such alliances he has given us a contemporary version of a once-familiar belief—that art can be a species of active virtue as well as a form of magic—and has thus sharply appealed to our sense of what man can be. Literary humanist qualities of this sort are not always easy to express today within the impersonal context of modern literary criticism—which tends, more and more, to ascribe virtue to structural performance within the text and to neglect what lies beyond. In fact, they are crucial virtues, and we fortunately have enough personal testimony—particularly from writers like Christopher Isherwood and Angus Wilson—to see the kind of inheritance he has left. At the same time, what Tony Tanner has called the "trace of totemism"[1] with which Forster has been and is still regarded—and I must assert here my own sense of indebtedness, intellectual, moral, and literary—has its dangers, and to his role and his influence may be ascribed certain slightly odd and uneasy features of Forster's present reputation. That he is a major writer I have no doubt, yet criticism has repeatedly expressed an unsureness about him, has wondered, time and time again, whether he really stands with the other great writers of the century we feel sure of—with Joyce or Conrad or Lawrence.

Why is this? One reason is surely that Forster stands much exposed to our modern predilection for historicist thinking—our inclination to substitute, in Karl Popper's phrase, "historical prophecy for conscience". Forster once told us that he belongs to "the fag-end of Victorian liberalism" (TC, 67), and the phrase is often taken with complete literalness and applied against him. As a result his intellectual and his literary destiny has been too readily linked with that strange death of liberal England which historians have dated around 1914, when the equation of economic individualism with social progress lost political force. Since it is easy to explain the exhaustion of political liberalism as a historical necessity, as the inevitable failure of a synthesis proven unworkable by the new social conditions of the second-stage Industrial Revolution, then it is also possible to see Forster's ideas and faith as historically superannuated, too. This view, indeed, has taken root—even though Forster recognises the ironies of the situation and works with them, even though he raises all the crucial questions about elevating social determinism above value; and we often overlook the fact that the liberalism he speaks for so obliquely has had a longer history as a moral conviction than as a political force, that

[1] Review of *The Cave and the Mountain* by Wilfred Stone, *London Magazine*, new series, VI, 5 (Aug. 1966), 102.

it has as much to do with our idea of man and culture as with our political solutions, that it speaks for a recurrent need for the criticism of institutions and collectivities from the standpoint of the claims of human wholeness. But coupled with this there has been another distrust: distrust of the entire idea of art and culture as Forster suggests or expresses it.

In this century critics have increasingly accepted modernist norms for the judgement of literature, even though, of course, many of our writers have not been modernists in the strict sense. Forster is a paradox here; he is, and he is not. There is in his work the appeal to art as transcendence, art as the one orderly product, a view that makes for modernism; and there is the view of art as a responsible power, a force for belief, a means of judgement, an impulse to spiritual control as well as spiritual curiosity. The point perhaps is that Forster is not, in the conventional sense, a modernist, but rather a central figure of the transition into modernism; and that is surely his interest, the force of his claim. He is, indeed, to a remarkable degree, the representative of two kinds of mind, two versions of literary possibility, and of the tensions of consciousness that exist between them. He stands at the beginning of the age of the new, speaking through it and against it. In this way his five novels—and particularly his last two—can be taken as reflecting the advantages and disadvantages of the humanist literary mind in an environment half hostile to it; they clearly and often painfully carry the strain of a direct encounter with new experience. Forster has been, by training and temperament, sufficiently the historian to see the irony: that culture itself is in history, that a humanist view of the arts as a way of sanely perceiving and evaluating is itself conditioned, for it has its own social environment and limits. So Forster is at once the spokesman for the transcendent symbol, the luminous wholeness of the work of art, out of time and in infinity, and for its obverse—the view that a proper part of art's responsibility is to know and live in the contingent world of history.

If Forster is indeed a Victorian liberal, as some of his critics charge, he is also deeply marked by the encounters that the moralised romantic inheritance must make with those environments which challenge it in matters of belief, technique, and aesthetics. Of course, Forster's confession that he belongs to the fag-end of Victorian liberalism does express a real inheritance; but that end is also the beginning of new forms of belief and of new literary postures and procedures. My point is that he emerges not as a conventionally modernist writer, but rather as a writer who has experienced the full impact of what modernism means— a hope for transcendence, a sense of apocalypse, an *avant-garde* posture, a sense of detachment, a feeling that a new phase of history has emerged—while retaining (with tentative balance that turns often to the ironic mode) much that modernism would affront.

Forster's traditional literary inheritance, which reaches back through the Victorian period to roots in English romanticism, is something which he himself has sketched clearly and well in books like *Marianne Thornton*. He has shown us the formative influence of the world of the Victorian upper-middle-class intelligentsia in its liberal radical mode—that world of "philanthropists, bishops, clergy, members of parliament, Miss Hannah More"[2] which reached into evangelical Christianity and into agnostic enlightenment, that world which he draws upon and values, and against which he also reacts. To the cultural historian, its interest lies in its unconditioned spirit, its sense of disinterestedness, its capacity to act beyond both self and class interest and to transcend its economic roots without losing its social standing. Its view of the critical intelligence working in society is therefore accompanied by no strong sense of disjunction, and it takes many of its terms from the moralised line of English romantic thought. What Forster inherits from it is apparent—something of the flavour of that engaging marriage made by the most influential English romantics, Wordsworth and Coleridge in particular, between the claims on the one hand of the imagination and the poet's transcendent vision, and on the other of right reason and moral duty; something of its power, therefore, to make a vision of Wholeness which embraces the social world in all its contingency. So the

[2] Macaulay, *op. cit.* (p. 45), p. 9.

personal connection between inner and outer worlds—a connection forged through the powers of passion and imagination—has its social equivalent, in the notion of an obligation on society that it, too, be whole; that it grant, as Mill stresses, "the absolute and essential importance of human development in its richest diverity",[3] that it sees, in Arnold's terms, that perfection can be both an *inward* condition of mind and spirit and a *general* expansion of the human family. Forster draws on the full equation for his fiction, taking as his proper field the social realm of action as well as the life of individuals in their personal relations, and criticising his characters and their society now from the standpoint of right reason and culture, now from that of the heart, the passions, the power of visionary imagination that can testify, however inadequately, to the claims of the infinite. Thus there come under fire "the vast armies of the benighted, who follow neither the heart nor the brain" (RV, 214); and the connective impulses embrace not only man and man, and man and infinity, but the social order, too.

But if Forster is undoubtedly an inheritor of that world of value, he inherits with a due sense of difficulty. In *Howards End* he touches in with deep force those powers and forces in history which are process, and can't be gainsaid; the pastoral and vividly felt landscape of England is turned by the demanding processes of urbanisation and industrialism into a civilisation of luggage; while the very economics of the intelligentsia he belongs to become a matter for ironic exposure. In *A Passage to India* the final nullity of romanticism is exposed in the cave, where the worlds within us and without echo together the sound of *boum*; this is the extreme beyond Coleridgean dejection, for the visionary hope is lost in the face of an unspeaking and utterly alien nature, a nature only self-reflecting. The will to vision and the liberal thrust to right reason, the desire to connect both with infinity and all mankind, are placed against unyielding forces in nature and history—obstructing the movement of Forster's visionary themes and producing,

[3] This phrase from Wilhelm von Humboldt, *Sphere and Duties of Government*, was used by J. S. Mill as his epigraph for *On Liberty* (1859).

particularly in these two last novels, a countervailing, ironic reaction. This countervailing sense, this sense of historical apocalypse coupled with spiritual abyss, is surely recognisably modernist. And what in the early novels appears as a species of social comedy—a comedy exercising the claims of moral realism against the liberal wish to draw clear lines between good and bad action—emerges in these latter novels as an essential irony of structure: indeed, as a direct challenge to the values Forster is so often supposed to represent. If, to cite Lionel Trilling (who writes so well of this ironic aspect of Forster), there is an ironic counterpart in the early work whereby while "the plot speaks of clear certainties, the manner resolutely insists that nothing can be quite so simple",[4] these complexities increase in the later work into the mental and aesthetic possession of two colliding views of the world.

Forster's way of assimilating two modes of thought—one an inheritance, the other an urgent group of ideas about contemporary necessity—is matched by the curious aesthetic implications of his techniques in fiction. He is often considered as a writer technically a coeval of his Victorian predecessors (Walter Allen calls him "a throwback"),[5] and in asserting his own debts has particularly named three writers: Jane Austen, Samuel Butler, and Marcel Proust. The indebtedness to the first two of his species of moralised social irony hardly needs elaborating; it is the third name which suggests that the "traditionalist" account of his technique is misleading. Of course, in his novels the omniscient author mediates, with the voice of the guide-book or essay or sermon, the proffered material—though as much to sustain fiction's place in the field of intelligence and thought as to establish the authenticity of fact. But at the same time he offers his work as the symbolist or autotelic artefact; a work of art is "the only material object in the universe which may possess internal harmony" (TC, 101). What is so fascinating about his most extended aesthetic statement, *Aspects of the Novel*, is its attempt to place the modes of symbolism and post-impressionism in the context of

[4] *E. M. Forster* (Hogarth Press, London, 1944), p. 13.
[5] *The English Novel* (Phoenix, London, 1954), p. 319.

what might be considered the more "traditional" story-telling function; the novel *tells* (rather than *is*) a story, and it lives in the conditioned world of stuff, of event, of history. (So, finally, Forster puts Tolstoy above Proust.) Yet it has transcendent purposes; art, "the one orderly product which our muddling race has produced" (*ibid.*), has Platonic powers to touch infinity, reach to the unity behind all things, prophesy (in the Shelleyan sense).

In this respect Forster is as post-impressionist or post-Paterian as anyone else in Bloomsbury, and the ultimate field of action for the arts is that of the "unseen". Procedurally this symbolist power seems to lie in the analogue with music, and is gained from aspects of the novel outside and beyond story, in thematic recurrences, leitmotifs, pattern and rhythm, prophetic song. The problem of whether art can redeem life by transcending it is crucial to modernism; the encounter between the formally transcendent—the epiphany, the unitary symbol—and the world of history recurs throughout its works. And Forster's view is, like that of most modernism, dualistic: art may reach beyond the world of men and things—the world of "story"—but it can never leave that world behind, and must seek meanings and connections in it. What distinguishes Forster is the faint hope which he entertains on behalf of history: the hope that by understanding and right relationship men may win for it a limited redemption.

I have suggested that Forster is deeply involved in some of the largest intellectual, cultural, and aesthetic collisions that occur in the transition into this century; and it is his sharp sense of the contingent, of the powers that rule the world of men, that makes him so. The result is a complex version of modern literary disquiet. An intermediary between those two literary traditions of "moderns" and "contemporaries" that Stephen Spender[6] sees as the two main lines of modern English writing, he bears these burdens so as to expose the crucial choices that a writer of this transitional period might make. Divided as he is between infinite and contingent, he is none the less more available to the offered pressures than most of the more confirmed modernists. This is

[6] *The Struggle of the Modern* (Hamish Hamilton, London, 1963).

because his sense of the "crisis" of infinity is so much bound up with his sense of the divisive and changing forces of the world of time. For he is increasingly concerned with the problems of the infinite view within the cultural movements of the modernising world; and in his growing sense of the need to synthesise an ever more eclectic experience he testifies to the new multiverse, the chaotic welter of values, which has confounded the modern mind. Hence his visions, though they may suggest an order or unity in the universe, are defined, increasingly from novel to novel, in terms of an anarchy that they must always comprehend. Thus they are never fully redemptive, since the world of time persistently enlarges our feelings of intellectual, moral, social, and spiritual relativism, creating a world in which no one philosophy or cosmology accounts for the world order—where it is possible to believe with Mrs. Moore that "Everything exists; nothing has value" (PI, 156). This, with its suggestion that in seeing life whole one may see nothing except multiplicity, is the obverse of the unitary vision; and in *A Passage to India*, his fullest and most eclectic book, Forster gives us in full that possibility—and its sources in social relations, personal relations, and the realm of spirit.

Forster may have an ideal of unity, a will to a whole solution, but we mistake him if we see only that in him. For he is characteristically not a novelist of solutions, but rather of reservations, of the contingencies and powers which inhibit spirit. The power of sympathy, understanding, and community with all things is for him an overriding power; but its claim to wholeness is always conditioned, and mystery, to which we must yield, co-exists with muddle, which we must try to redeem, or even accept in its nullity. Indeed, it is because Forster is so attentive to the forces in our culture and world-order which induce the vision of anarchy —and threaten through its very real powers not only the will to but the very insights of the whole vision—that he seems so central a writer; a novelist whom we in our turn have not always seen whole.

Forster is a difficult and ambiguous writer, a writer who has often made his critics uneasy and caused them to feel how strangely elusive his work is. His observation of his materials, and his way of making his structures, usually involves two tones that come into perplexing relationship. There is the instinct towards "poetry", which goes with the view of art as a symbolist unity; and there is the comedy and the irony, the belittling aspect of his tone, which brings in the problems and difficulties of the contingent world. Because of this it is often possible simultaneously to interpret his work positively and negatively, depending on the kind of critical attentiveness one gives.

Thus for some critics, like Wilfred Stone, *A Passage to India* is Forster's most affirmative and optimistic novel, the one which most suggests, as Stone puts it, that "unity and harmony are the ultimate promises of life."[7] "The theme which this book hammers home," says Stone, "is that, for all our differences, we are in fact *one*. . . . Physically of one environment, we are also psychically one, and it is reason's denial of our commonality, the repression of that *participation mystique*, which has caused man to rule his Indias and himself with such futility and blindness."[8] But other critics like James McConkey and Alan Wilde have come to precisely the opposite view, seeing the work as a novel of the final dissociation between the chaotic life of man and an intractable eternal reality. In part the decision depends upon whether one insists, like Trilling, on a relatively realistic reading of the book, or whether, as E. K. Brown does, one reads it as a "symbolist" novel. If the world of men and manners, of politics and human behaviour, which it depicts suggests divisiveness, the world of the work itself as single "orderly product" suggests profound correspondences within it, a power to resolve its meanings which lies beyond any given character. Of this aspect of the book, Frank Kermode has remarked that it depends upon faking—faking a universe of promised wholeness, of rhetorical and structural unity, of a testing of the world of men from the standpoint of total coherence: "All that civilisation excepts or disconnects has

[7] Stone, *op. cit.* (p. 19), p. 344.
[8] *ibid.*, p. 339.

to be got in for meaning to subsist."[9] What this means is that the
world of men and the world of order must exist in paradoxical
relationship, and this is what Lionel Trilling seems to imply, too,
when he remarks that the novel has an unusual imbalance between
plot and story: "The characters are of sufficient size for the plot;
they are not large enough for the story—and that indeed is the
point of the story."[10] But it is typically in such contrasts of time
and transcendence that Forster deals, and to clarify the relationship between them one needs to look very closely at the overall
working of the novel.

To a considerable extent, the book deals in themes and matters
we have learned to associate with Forster from his previous
novels. Here again are those rival claims upon men and nature
which dichotomise the universe—the claims of the seen and the
unseen, the public and the private, the powers of human activities
and institutions and of the ultimate mysteries for which the right
institutions and activities have yet to be found. And here again
Forster's own sympathies are relatively apparent. The book is
focused upon the testing-field of human relationships, with their
various possibilities and disasters; on the "good will plus culture
and intelligence" (p. 65) which are the necessary conditions of
honest intercourse; on the clashes of interest and custom which
divide men but which the liberal mind must hope, as Fielding
hopes, to transcend. Its modes of presentation are familiarly complex—moving between a "poetic" evocation of the world of
mystery and a "comic" evocation of the world of muddle,
which is in a sense its obverse and refers to the normal state of
men.

But what is unmistakable, I think, is that in this book Forster
reveals new powers and resources—of a kind not previously
achieved in his fiction—and that this extension of resource is
linked with an extension of his sensibility, and above all with a new
sense of complexity. For instance, *A Passage to India* is not simply

[9] "The One Orderly Product (E. M. Forster)", *Puzzles and Epiphanies*
(Routledge, London, 1962), p. 84.
[10] Trilling, *op. cit.*, p. 126.

an international novel—in the Jamesian sense of attempting to resolve contrasting value-systems by means of a cosmopolitan scale of value—but a global novel. The contrast of England and India is not the end of the issue, since India is schismatic within itself; India's challenge is the challenge of the multiverse, a new version of the challenge that Henry Adams faced on looking at the dynamo. What the city is as metaphor in *Howards End*, India is in *Passage*; it is a metaphor of contingency. Forster is not simply interested in raising the social-comic irony of confronting one social world with the standards of another; he stretches through the social and political implications to religious and mystical ones, and finally to the most basic question of all—how, in the face of such contingency, one structures meaning.

The geographical scale of the novel is, in short, supported by a vast scale of standpoint. Forster attempts a structure inclusive of the range of India, and the judgements of the book are reinforced by the festivals and rituals of three religions, by the heterodoxy— racial, political, cultural, religious, and mystical—of this multiple nation, and by the physical landscape of a country which both invites meaning ("Come, come") and denies any. "Nothing embraces the whole of India, nothing, nothing," says Aziz (PI, 151); the landscape and the spirit of the earth divide men ("Trouble after trouble encountered him [Aziz], because he had challenged the spirit of the Indian earth, which tries to keep men in compartments" (p. 133)); and even the sects are divided within themselves just as the earth is:

> The fissures in the Indian soil are infinite: Hinduism, so solid from a distance, is riven into sects and clans, which radiate and join, and change their names according to the aspect from which they are approached. (p. 304.)

Forster's social comedy works to provoke, among a variety of different and sympathetically viewed groups, those ironic international and intra-national encounters that come when one value-system meets another and confusion and muddle ensue. But his other aim is to call up, by a poetic irradiation, the ironies lying within the forces of mystery and muddle in the constituted universe of nature itself. For here, too, are deceptions, above all in the absence of Beauty, which is traditionally a form for infinity, so that the very discourse of Romanticism becomes negative under the hot sun—who is "not the unattainable friend, either of men or birds or other suns, [who] was not the eternal promise, the never-withdrawn suggestion that haunts our consciousness; he was merely a creature, like the rest, and so debarred from glory" (p. 120). There is much in India that invites a cosmic meaning, but it places both man and infinity:

> Trees of a poor quality bordered the road, indeed the whole scene was inferior, and suggested that the countryside was too vast to admit of excellence. In vain did each item in it call out, "Come, come." There was not enough god to go round. The two young people conversed feebly and felt unimportant. (p. 92.)

All this stretches the Whitmanesque enterprise called up by the title to a vast level of inclusiveness. It also involves Forster in a placing of the social and human world of his novel in a way he has never approached before. One way of putting the situation is to say that the human plot of the novel is set into singular relation to the verbal plot, with its radiating expansiveness of language. The human plot of the novel is essentially a story hinging on Adela Quested, who comes to India to marry, has doubts about her marriage when she sees what India has made of her fiancé, and tries herself to create a more reasonable relationship between British and Indians. She takes part in an expedition, arranged by an Indian, to the Marabar caves, in one of which she believes she is attacked by him. She accuses him of attempted rape, and, although at the trial she retracts her accusation, the incident has sown dissent and discord, and has exposed the political and institutional tensions of the country.

The plot moves us from the world of personal relationships to the social world (which in this case involves political relationships), and is set largely in and around the city of Chandrapore, at a time not stated but evidently intended to be in the 1920s.[11] The dense social world that Forster delinates so skilfully consists primarily of racial or religious groups with their own customs and patterns. The English, whom we see largely through the eyes of Adela Quested and Mrs. Moore, visiting India together, are identified with their institutional functions. Mostly professional middle-class people, they have gone through a process of adaptation to their duties, which are, as Ronnie says, "to do justice and keep the peace" (p. 53). They have learned the importance of solidarity, conventions, rank, and standoffishness; and their judgements and their social order are those of a particular class in a particular situation. Their ethics are dutiful and serious; they have a deep sense of rational justice; they are distrustful of mysticism and lethargy; their deep Englishness has been reinforced by their situation. They operate at the level of political and social duty, and their relationships—the ties that bind the characters together and enable Forster to thread the way from one to another—are those of the political and social roles they play.

The other group, which we see first largely through the eyes of Aziz, consists of Indians, though these are themselves divided by religions and castes. Here again what we see are primarily the professional classes, linked to the British by their duties and to their own people by their familial and friendly relationships. The two main groupings that emerge here are, of course, the Hindus and the Moslems, and Forster differentiates carefully between them, and their respective versions of India. Where they differ radically from the English is in their long and adaptive response to the confusions of their country, a response which obscures the firm lines of value that the British in their isolation can protect, and permits lethargy, emotionalism, and mysticism. Forster

---

[11] Rose Macaulay finds it to be earlier: "the date of the novel is apparently approximately that of the earlier visit. . . . The European war is still ahead." (*Op. cit.*, pp. 176, 186.) Forster disagrees: the war Aziz foresees is the Second World War (PI, Everyman's Library ed., Dent, London, repr. 1957, p. ix). But Rose Macaulay's point has an imaginative truth: the book comes out of two phases of Imperial India.

explores Indian custom and faith in great detail, noting its own patterns of classification, its own way of making and not making social and moral distinctions, above all recognising that Indians have adapted to a different physical environment by being comprehensive or passive rather than orderly or rationalistic.

These worlds—Anglo-Indian (to use the phrase of the day), Hindu, Moslem—are given us in full as they connect and draw apart, and Forster enters imaginatively into each of them. And to a large extent what interests him is not the relations between people, the normal matter for the novelist, but their separation. In the novel's social scenes we are always conscious of those who are absent, and much of the discussion in the early part of the novel is devoted to those not present—the whites are talked of by the Indians, the Indians by the whites. And this suggests the vast social inclusiveness of the novel, which spreads beyond the communities established for the sake of the action into a cast of thousands: nameless marginal characters who appear for a moment and are gone, like the punkah wallah or the voice out of the darkness at the club, and the inhabitants of Chandrapore who seem made "of mud moving" (p. 9).

Out of this complex social world derives a complex moral world, in which the values of no one group are given total virtue. The English may have thrown the net of rationalism and "civilisation" over the country, but India's resistance to this—"The triumphant machine of civilisation may suddenly hitch and be immobilised into a car of stone" (p. 220)—puts them in ironic relation to Indian reality; they scratch only the surface of its life, and theirs is a feeble invasion. On the other hand, the passive comprehensiveness of India is seen as itself a kind of social decay, debased as well as spiritual, leading to a potential neglect of man. The traditional repositories of Forsterian virtue—goodwill plus culture and intelligence—function only incompletely in this universe; and Forster's own liberal passion for social connection motivates a large section of the action, but does not contain its chief interest. In the deceptively guide-bookish opening chapter

Forster establishes an appeal beyond the social world, to the over-arching sky; it looks, at first, like a figure for the potential unity of man, the redemption that might come through breaking out of the social institutions and classifications that segregate them into their closed groupings, but the gesture has an ambiguous quality. The civil station "shares nothing with the city except the overarching sky" (p. 10), but the sky itself is an infinite mystery, and reaching away into its "farther distance, . . . beyond colour, last freed itself from blue" (p. 11). Certainly, beyond the world of social organisation is that world of "the secret understanding of the heart" (p. 22) to which Aziz appeals; this is the world that is damaged when Ronnie and Mrs. Moore discuss Aziz and she finds: "Yes, it was all true, but how false as a summary of the man; the essential life of him had been slain." (p. 37.)

Forster is, as usual, superb at creating that "essential life" and showing what threatens it, and much of the book deals with its virtues and its triumphs. So at one level the social world *is* re-deemed by those who resist its classifications—by Adela and Mrs. Moore, Fielding, Aziz, Godbole. Forster does not belittle their victories directly except in so far as he sees their comedy. But he does place beyond them a world of infinitude which is not, here, to be won through the personal. For this is not the entire realm of moral victory in the novel; indeed, these acts of resistance, which provide the book's lineal structure, are usually marked by failure. Adela's is a conventional disaster; she makes the moral mistake of exposing the personal to the social. Fielding's is more compli-cated; he is an agent of liberal contact through goodwill plus culture and intelligence, but he, like Mrs. Moore, meets an echo:

"In the old eighteenth century, when cruelty and injustice raged, an invisible power repaired their ravages. Everything echoes now; there's no stopping the echo. The original sound may be harmless, but the echo is always evil." This reflection about an echo lay at the verge of Fielding's mind. He could never develop it. It belonged to the universe that he had missed or rejected. And the mosque missed it too. Like himself, those shallow arcades provided but a limited asylum. (pp. 286–7.)

As for Mrs. Moore, who does touch it, she encounters another force still—the moral nihilism that comes when the boundary walls are down. Her disaster dominates the novel, for it places even moral and mystical virtue within the sphere of contingency; it, too, is subject to spiritual anarchy. Beyond the world of the plot, the lineal world of consequences and relationships, there lies a second universe of fictional structure, which links spiritual events, and then a third, which in turn places these in history and appeals to the infinite recession of the universe beyond any human structure that seeks to comprehend it.

This we may see by noting that in this novel, as compared with the earlier ones, the world of men is clearly granted reduced powers. The universe of time and contingency is made smaller, by the nature that surrounds man, by the scale of the continent on which man's presence is a feeble invasion, by the sky which over-arches him and his works. It is a world of dwarfs and of dwarfed relationships, in which the familiar forces of romantic redemption in Forster's work—personal relationships as mirrors to infinity, a willingness to confront the unseen—undertake their movements toward connection without the full support of the universe. The theme recurs, but Mrs. Moore expresses it most strongly in Chapter XIV, when she reflects on her situation and grows towards her state of spiritual nullity in the cave:

> She felt increasingly (vision or nightmare?) that, though people are important, the relations between them are not, and that in particular too much fuss has been made over marriage; centuries of carnal embracement, yet man is no nearer to understanding man. And today she felt this with such force that it seemed itself a relationship, itself a person who was trying to take hold of her hand. (p. 141.)

The negative withdrawal is, of course, an aspect of that "twilight of the double vision in which so many elderly people are involved" (p. 216), and it is not the only meaning in the book. But it is the dominant one. It is by seeking its obverse that Adela compounds her basic moral error:

> It was Adela's faith that the whole stream of events is important
> and interesting, and if she grew bored she blamed herself severely
> and compelled her lips to utter enthusiasms. This was the only
> insincerity in a character otherwise sincere, and it was indeed the
> intellectual protest of her youth. She was particularly vexed now
> because she was both in India and engaged to be married, which
> double event should have made every instant sublime. (p. 139.)

Human relationships are dwarfed not only by the scale of the
historical and social world, which is potentially redeemable, but
by the natural world, which is not.

Of course, intimations of transcendence are present throughout
the novel. Structurally they run through the seasonal cycle, from
divisive hot sun to the benedictive healing water at the end, and
from Mosque to Caves to Temple. By taking that as his order,
Forster is able poetically to sustain the hope of a spiritual possibility, a prefiguring of the world beyond in the world below. The
climax of this theme is Godbole's attempt at "completeness, not
reconstruction" (p. 298). But what happens here is that divine
revelation is shifted to the level of the comic sublime; Forster's
rhetoric now puts what has been spiritually perplexing—the webs,
nets, and prisons that divide spirit as well as society—back into the
comic universe of muddle. The Mau festival is the celebration of
the formlessness of the Indian multiverse, seen for a moment in-
clusively. The poetic realm of the novel, in which above all Mrs.
Moore and Godbole have participated, and which has dominated
the book's primary art, is reconciled with the muddle of the world
of men, in an emotional cataract that momentarily repairs the
divisions of the spiritual world (through Godbole's revelation)
and the social world (through the festival itself). It satisfies much
of the passion for inclusiveness that has been one thread in the
novel, the desire that heaven should include all because India *is* all.
Earlier the two Christian missionaries have disagreed: Mr. Sorley,
the more advanced,

admitted that the mercy of God, being infinite, may well embrace all mammals. And the wasps? He became uneasy during
the descent to wasps, and was apt to change the conversation.
And oranges, cactuses, crystals and mud? and the bacteria inside
Mr. Sorley? No, no, this is going too far. We must exclude someone from our gathering, or we shall be left with nothing. (p. 41.)

Godbole's universe of spirit is much more inclusive:

> Godbole consulted the music-book, said a word to the drummer,
> who broke rhythm, made a thick little blur of sound, and pro-
> duced a new rhythm. This was more exciting, the inner images it
> evoked more definite, and the singers' expressions became fatuous
> and languid. They loved all men, the whole universe, and scraps
> of their past, tiny splinters of detail, emerged for a moment to
> melt into the universal warmth. Thus Godbole, though she was
> not important to him, remembered an old woman he had met in
> Chandrapore days. Chance brought her into his mind while it
> was in this heated state, he did not select her, she happened to
> occur among the throng of soliciting images, a tiny splinter, and
> he impelled her by his spiritual force to that place where com-
> pleteness can be found. Completeness, not reconstruction. His
> senses grew thinner, he remembered a wasp seen he forgot where,
> perhaps on a stone. He loved the wasp equally, he impelled it
> likewise, he was imitating God. And the stone where the wasp
> clung—could he . . . no, he could not, he had been wrong to
> attempt the stone, logic and conscious effort had seduced, he
> came back to the strip of red carpet and discovered that he was
> dancing upon it. (p. 298.)

His doctrine—"completeness, not reconstruction"—is, of course,
a species of transcendence, a momentary vision of the whole, the
invocation of a universe invested with spirit. It links up with the
symbolist plot of the novel, its power as a radiant image, rather
than with plot in the linear sense, with its world of "and then . . .
and then . . ." Threading its way through the novel, to an old
woman and a wasp, it takes these "soliciting images" and puts
them in new association—not with all things, but with each other
and with what else comes almost unbidden into the world of
spirit. But the stone is left, and equally spirit may or may not

invest the universe in any of its day-to-day affairs: "Perhaps all these things! Perhaps none!" (p. 302.) Things, in freeing themselves from their traditional associations, social and historical, form a new order, beyond dialogue, beyond human plot, in the realm where poetic figures function on their own order of consciousness. Yet here, too, irony is at work: mystery is sometimes muddle, completeness is sometimes the universe where "everything exists, nothing has value" (p. 156). If history ultimately obstructs, and does not give us a final, rounded structure in terms of human events, if the horses, the earth, the clutter of human institutions say, "No, not yet," then like obstructions dwell in the realm of spirit and symbol, too: the sky says, "No, not there". (p. 336.)

The linear, social plot, then, has stretched a long way in search of a structure of its own that will provide coherence in the world, but if it finds one it is in the form of an oblique, doubtful and ironic promise; personal relations only go so far to solve the muddle of history. As for the symbolist plot, it transcends but it does not redeem; it is there but "neglects to come" (p. 84). The power of the novel lies, of course, in the Whitmanesque ambition to include multitudes, to find eternity in some order in the given world. But is this ambition realised? Intimations of eternity may have their symbols in the world of men (in love and relationship) and in the world of nature (in the force of mystery that resides in things); the social and the natural worlds have in them touches that promise wholeness. But they do not of themselves have unity; they are themselves afflicted by the double vision which is all that man can bring to them, grounded as he is in history and hope at once. The world stretches infinitely about us, and there is infinity beyond us. But questions bring us only to the unyielding hostility of the soil and the unyielding ambiguity of the sky.

The universe, then, is less intimation than cipher; a mask rather than a revelation in the romantic sense. Does love meet with love? Do we receive but what we give? The answer is surely a paradox, the paradox that there are Platonic universals beyond, but that the glass is too dark to see them. Is there a light beyond the glass, or

is it a mirror only to the self? The Platonic cave is even dark
than Plato made it, for it introduces the echo, and so leaves
back in the world of men, which does not carry total meaning,
just a story of events. The Platonic romantic gesture of the mat
in the cave is the dominating ambiguity of the book. Does it see
itself in the polished wall of stone, or is the glimmer of radiance a
promise?

> There is little to see, and no eye to see it, until the visitor arrives
> for his five minutes, and strikes a match. Immediately another
> flame rises in the depths of the rock and moves towards the surface
> like an imprisoned spirit: the walls of the circular chamber have
> been most marvellously polished. The two flames approach and
> strive to unite, but cannot, because one of them breathes air, the
> other stone. A mirror inlaid with lovely colours divides the
> lovers, delicate stars of pink and grey interpose, exquisite
> nebulae, shadings fainter than the tail of a comet or the midday
> moon, all the evanescent life of the granite, only here visible.
> Fists and fingers thrust above the advancing soil—here at last is
> their skin, finer than any covering acquired by the animals,
> smoother than windless water, more voluptuous than love. The
> radiance increases, the flames touch one another, kiss, expire. The
> cave is dark again, like all the caves. (pp. 130–1.)

Isn't it less the transcendence of a Whitman, uniting all things
through the self and the ongoing lines of history, than the ambiguous and narcissistic transcendence of Melville, where the universe
is a diabolical cipher, where the desire to penetrate meaning ends
only in our being swallowed up in the meaning we have con-
ferred? Isn't the novel not Forster's "Passage to India", but
rather, in the end, Forster's *Moby Dick*?

Forster's "Wobblings": The Manuscripts of *A Passage to India*

by Oliver Stallybrass

E. M. Forster once referred to the "satisfaction" with which "experts in psychology, and collectors, and researchers into the process of creation" regard the "wobblings of authors" as exhibited in their manuscripts.[1] These people, or those of them within striking distance of Austin, Texas, have since 1960 been able to extend their satisfaction to Forster's own "wobblings"; for in that year the Humanities Research Center at the University of Texas acquired from the London Library all the extant manuscripts of *A Passage to India*. Since 1965 some of this satisfaction has been available also to anybody with the patience to unravel Robert L. Harrison's ingeniously tangled skein of *textus receptus* and manuscript variants.[2]

---

[1] *The Library*, series 5, vol. XIII (1958), pp. 142–3. Forster was reviewing *Authors at Work: an address delivered by Robert H. Taylor at the opening of an exhibition of literary manuscripts at the Grolier Club together with a catalogue of the exhibition by Herman W. Liebert and facsimiles of many of the exhibits* (New York, 1957).

[2] *The Manuscripts of* A Passage to India (University Microfilms, Ann Arbor, Mich., 1965), referred to in this essay as MPI.

This account of the manuscripts may appropriately start with the circumstances in which they crossed the Atlantic. In 1960 the London Library, faced with acute financial difficulties, hit on the idea of an auction sale, all the objects to be sold being specially presented by members and well-wishers of the Library. E. M. Forster had been a life member since 1904 and a committee member from 1933 to 1948, and had once described the Library as catering "neither for the goose nor for the rat, but for creatures who are trying to be human. The desire to know more, the desire to feel more, and, accompanying these but not strangling them, the desire to help others: here, briefly, is the human aim, and the Library exists to further it." (TC, 313–14.) Now he underlined these memorable words by presenting the manuscripts of his masterpiece. They formed the sale's *pièce de résistance*, and at £6,500 established a new record price for a manuscript by a living author.

At that time I happened to be Chief Cataloguer at the London Library; but my cataloguing activities were restricted, during one of the happiest months of my life, to producing the draft of a single entry for the Christie sale catalogue. This rate of progress is not quite as reprehensible as it may seem: the more than 500 pieces of paper of all shapes and sizes arrived in no discernible order, often had totally unrelated matter on their two sides, and altogether formed a gigantic jigsaw puzzle, some of whose pieces, Forster suggested in a letter, "you may feel tempted to lose". Piety prevailed, however, and only two blank pieces of paper and a few rusty paper-clips were discarded.

As publicity for the sale I had been encouraged to write a newspaper article on the manuscripts, and this appeared in *The Guardian*, 20 June 1960. In writing it I assembled much more material than I was able to incorporate in 1,000 words, and it is this material, checked and revised in the light of Harrison's indispensable work, which forms the basis of the present essay. The only other published account of the manuscripts, apparently, apart from Harrison's own Introduction with its chapter-by-chapter commentary, is an appendix in George H. Thomson's *The Fiction of E. M.*

Forster.[3] This is a valuable study, but its emphases are closely related to a particular interpretation of the novel, and there is room for a more general account of the manuscripts.

I use the plural advisedly: for the first fact to emerge clearly, when I began my sorting operations, was that I was dealing not only with the "final" manuscript, but with a large quantity of earlier draft material as well. The second discovery was the need for those quotation marks round "final". The word has to be used, since Forster insists that there was no later manuscript; but it blurs the remarkable divergence between the manuscripts and the published version, between the jigsaw puzzle and the picture on the lid.

There were, in these circumstances, at least two possible assembly methods open to me. The one I chose was to start by assembling a version which should be (*a*) as complete and (*b*) as late, i.e. as close to the published text, as possible. In most cases there was no conflict between these two aims; but occasionally I had to use my judgement in assigning priority to one or the other. Thus, where an accidental gap of a mere three words could be avoided only by substituting an earlier version of the page in question, it seemed reasonable to accept the tiny gap; where, on the other hand, two consecutive pages of the generally latest version included, on the back of one, a later draft of one sentence of the other, it would have been absurd to reject a complete page for the sake of one sentence.

At the end of this stage I had assembled a version of the novel which, though written (as we shall see) over a decade and containing some inconsistencies, notably over names, is virtually continuous and complete. Many passages present in the published version are absent there—and vice versa—but of definite lacunae there are only six, all minor ones. Three are caused by the loss of, probably, one leaf in each case, and two by the imperfect dove-

[3] Wayne State University Press, Detroit, 1967, pp. 261–72. John Colmer has also made use of the manuscripts, or rather of Harrison's edition of them, in *E. M. Forster: A Passage to India* (Arnold, London, 1967).

tailing of an interpolated passage; while the sixth, already mentioned, represents a mere three words inadvertently omitted in
rewriting.

Physically, this version consists of 399 single leaves, mostly
folio or double folio torn in two—though sixty-six leaves have
been reduced to a variety of sizes by the author's habit of tearing
off, usually at the bottom, material which has been rewritten on
another leaf. It is important to note that Forster, in this novel at
any rate, never continues on the verso of a leaf, but always on a
new recto. Nevertheless, eighty of these 399 leaves bear some
writing on their versos. In a very few cases a passage has been
written on a verso for interpolation in the following recto; in a
few others a verso contains a *later version* of part of the following
recto; and a few versos contain working notes or even, occasionally, extraneous matter, such as two fragments (MPI, 725) of what
Forster has identified as abortive attempts at short stories. The
great majority, however, of these eighty used versos contain discarded draft material, sometimes deleted, sometimes not. In most
cases these early drafts on what are now to be regarded as versos
relate to the same general area of the book as their rectos, but
there are some notable exceptions (e.g. MPI, 452–3).

It will make for ease of reference if I adopt the terms used by
the Humanities Research Center[4] and by Harrison (both of whom
appear to have found my classification acceptable),[5] and refer to
the main manuscript, just described, as MS. A. MS. B is the name
given to the 101 remaining folio manuscripts leaves, including
nineteen with versos utilised, which represent in the main variants
of passages found in the rectos, and sometimes also the versos, of
MS. A. Between MS. B and the versos of MS. A there seems to be
no radical distinction—merely the fortuitous one of which discarded leaves came to Forster's hand, and at what stage. Indeed,

[4] To whose Director and staff I am grateful for answering some of my
many questions.
[5] Harrison, indeed, appears to endow MS. A with a more unitary
status than it possesses when he suggests that "the direction of the
book was fairly well established at the time of writing MS. A" (MPI,
xix). I return later to the complicated question of chronology.

one continuous fragment (MPI, 693–7) consists of A387v, B97, A388v, A393v, and B98, and illustrates neatly the problem of classification and the value of Harrison's work in reuniting fragments which I was forced to sunder.

With MS. B my method was to assemble the longest possible continuous passages, and arrange these in the order of their starting-points, in so far as I could determine these with any precision in relation either to MS. A or to the published book. No doubt some of my decisions were arbitrary, and in at least one case (B11; MPI 244–5) mistaken; in another (B59; MPI, 239 and 328–9) it looks as if at some stage a leaf has got turned over so that as regards its "recto", though not its "verso", it is badly misplaced.

In addition to the manuscripts proper there is a typescript carbon of nineteen quarto sheets known as MS. C. This includes a discarded epigraph to Part I,[6] but consists mainly of a version, intermediate between MS. A and the published book, of various passages, the longest being from Chapter XXXVI;[7] also a typescript half-title page with autograph dedication, and a handwritten title-page which is clearly related to the typescript, and of which I shall have more to say.

Finally there are four folded double folio leaves of corrections and addenda, to which likewise I shall return.

As we have seen, a feature of the version represented by the rectos of MS. A in their final state (and *a fortiori* of earlier versions) is its wide divergence from the published text. Chapter XXXII is unique in diverging only by one word, while a few others, notably

---

[6] The epigraph, of which another version is found on A32v, reads:

Four men went to pray.
The first said to the Muezzin, "Surely it is not the hour for prayer yet?"
The second said to the first, "Do not blame the Muezzin."
The third said to the second, "Do not blame him for blaming the Muezzin."
The fourth said, "Thank God, I am not as these other three."
The prayers of all four were unheard.

Jalaluddin Rumi

[7] Chapter numbers refer to the published book, not the manuscripts.

I and XXVII–XXXI, offer only minor variants. Elsewhere, not only do the division and even the order of chapters vary—in MS.A Chapter VII precedes Chapters V and VI—but the entire text shows so many changes that but for Forster's statement to the contrary it would be tempting to postulate a later manuscript version between this one and the author's typescript, which seems to have constituted the final copy.

Instead, Forster must have made extensive alterations, either in producing the typescript, or on the typescript, or both. There are, in fact, several pieces of evidence which between them show clearly that he did both: the state of a number of the typescript leaves; the four leaves containing notes, some precise, others less so ("the whole of this Ch [i.e. XIII] . . . is not quite right"), of alterations, made or about to be made, on the numbered typescript pages; and those places (MPI, 4, for example) where, it seems, Forster grew dissatisfied while typing a page, and redrafted a sentence or two on the preceding verso. That he also retyped some leaves from a corrected carbon copy, and sent the new leaves to the publisher at a late stage, is suggested by two typescript leaves of MS.C which, though different from the book, have evidently been in the hands of the publisher or even of the printer; and this hypothesis is confirmed by other evidence, for which I am indebted to Mr. B. W. Fagan, among the records of the London publisher, Edward Arnold. Yet another indication of the complex operations involved in the production of this novel is the handwritten title-page (MS. C), the joint work of author and publisher, bearing a pencilled note in the author's hand: "*Uncorrected Typescript*. N.B. *Edith* Quested becomes *Adela* about page 40. *Khan* Bahadur *Nawab* Bahadur in Ch XX"—a note which suggests, among other things, that the earlier chapters were probably typed out before the later ones were written.

This leads to the question of chronology. The author stated at one point "Green ink chapters written *c.* 1913. Adela as Edith or Janet. Ronnie [*sic*] as Gerald. Rest written 1922–1923", but later agreed that this description is not quite accurate. First, Ronny Heaslop, while his surname varies, nowhere appears as Gerald, though among the extraneous material another Gerald crops up, in what is conceivably a draft fragment of *The Longest Journey* (MPI, 724–5). Second, the last page of the manuscript is dated January 21st, 1924. Finally, the green-ink-black-ink distinction needs modifying. The chapters written entirely or substantially in green ink are I–VII (Chapter II having in black ink eight octavo leaves evidently written at the same period as the rest, and one short interpolated passage); in addition there are green-ink leaves in the main manuscript of Chapter XII, and among the supplementary material for Chapters VIII, XII and XIV. Now, it seems unlikely that after a decade the author should again have been using green ink, but spasmodically this time instead of consistently. On the other hand, parts at least of the manuscript of Chapter VIII, being based on a story about an animal charging a car which the author heard during his second visit to India in 1921[8] (the first had been in 1912–13), must date from the later period. Graphology might settle the question, but other evidence —watermarks, the political flavour of a paragraph in Chapter IX (PI, 111), and the appearance in Chapter VIII, for the first time and in full measure, of truncated leaves[9]—suggest that it would be more correct to say "Chapter I–VII and subsequent green-ink leaves written *c.* 1913, rest written 1922 or 1923 to 1924". In this case, eleven leaves are all that remain of the earlier version for Chapters VIII–XIV; though it is possible that Chapters IX–XI, which are not essential from a structural point of view, had no existence until the later period. The interesting points in any case are the long interval, and the fact that each creative period followed a visit to India.

Apart from a few pages which are evidently fair copies, the manuscripts are untidy. Mention has already been made of the

[8] See PI, Everyman's Library ed., Dent, London, repr. 1957, p. xxix; and HD, 89–90.

[9] This habit of decapitating (or more commonly depeditating) partially rewritten leaves, in order to use the versos of the discarded segments, may have been acquired under wartime conditions in Egypt; the late H. E. Wortham, who edited the *Egyptian Mail* at the time, told me that Forster's contributions were often written on the backs of envelopes.

various sizes to which many leaves have been reduced. Sometimes the matter discarded in this way has first been deleted, sometimes not, and, since the tear is often roughly made, occasional undeleted but redundant words are to be found. There is much deletion and correction, some of it in pencil, and, to quote the author again, "scriggles . . . surge up from the margin, they extend tentacles, they interbreed."[10] Apart from "scriggles", the margins contain occasional dates (unreliable: two consecutive dates in Chapter XX read 9/7/23 and 10/6/23), tallies of words, and question marks, some of which suggest factual points to be verified, others perhaps a vague dissatisfaction. A few chapters have their pages numbered in pencil, but the majority have only what appears to be an indication of how many pages they contain, or once contained, while the numbering of the chapters themselves is erratic and shows traces of alteration, some of it done by the author immediately before delivery to the London Library. As for the actual handwriting, this undoubtedly comes into the category of "cacography if there is such a word".[10] (There is.)

The main impression conveyed by the manuscripts, and by their divergences from the book, is of an author who writes fast, and uses the physical act of writing as part of "the process of creation", not as a mere recording technique. Speed would account for some curious spelling mistakes and for such slips as "service" for "surface", "break" for "brake", "their" for "there", and "parents' pupils" for "pupils' parents" (MPI, 79)—this last, it is amusing to note, occurring in three other fragments (MPI, 39, 40, 42) as a deliberately introduced slip of the tongue. It is fascinating to compare these first and final versions—some passages have as many as five drafts—and to see a touch of irony added, a wrong note eliminated, an inert snatch of dialogue springing suddenly to life. An author's "improvements" are not always accepted as such by all his readers—Henry James is a case in point—but few are likely to quarrel with the judgement revealed in the following changes:

[10] *The Library, loc. cit.*

". . . Mrs. Turton takes bribes, red-nose is apparently still a bachelor." (MPI, 8.)
". . . *Mrs. Turton takes bribes, Mrs. Red-nose does not and cannot, because so far there is no Mrs. Red-nose.*" (PI, 13.)

. . . a family marriage that had been celebrated with imperfect solemnity. (MPI, 12.)
. . . *a family circumcision that had been celebrated with imperfect pomp.* (PI, 15.)[11]

". . . the verandah is good enough for an Indian and Mrs. Callander takes my carriage and cuts me dead. . . ." (MPI, 28; Aziz is speaking.)
". . . *the verandah is good enough for an Indian, yes, yes, let him stand, and Mrs. Callendar takes my carriage and cuts me dead. . . .*" (PI, 25.)

. . . in case the natives should see the Englishwomen acting . . . . (MPI, 35.)
. . . *lest the servants should see their mem-sahibs acting. . . .* (PI, 26.)

One touch of regret—not conversational regret, but the stab that goes down to the soul—would have made him a different man, and she would have worshipped him. (MPI, 89.)
One touch of regret—not the canny substitute but the true regret from the heart—would have made him a different man, and the British Empire a different institution. (PI, 54.)

He was inaccurate because he desired to honour her. (MPI, 343.)
He was inaccurate because he desired to honour her, and—facts being entangled—he had to arrange them in her vicinity, as one tidies the ground after extracting a weed. (PI, 165.)

. . . he chose to pretend that Mr. Das had a sense of justice equal to his own. (MPI, 471.)
. . . *he liked to maintain that his old Das really did possess moral courage of the Public School brand.* (PI, 224.)

Her particular brand of sensations and opinions—why should they claim so much importance in the world? (MPI, 476.)
Her particular brand of opinions, and the suburban Jehovah who sanctified them—by what right did they claim so much importance in the world, and assume the title of civilisation? (PI, 226–7.)

[11] This alteration may reflect the difference between what was felt mentionable in print in 1913 and in 1923; just as the omission, on which Forster himself has commented (AH, 173–4), from the second edition of *Sense and Sensibility* of a sentence containing the words "natural daughter" reflected a change in the opposite direction.

One could multiply such examples endlessly. In addition, there is a general tendency to convert narrative into dialogue—though occasionally the reverse happens, as when "a shapeless discussion occurred" (PI, 47) replaces the actual discussion (MPI, 72)—and to eliminate explanatory comment of the "he was lying" type (MPI, 607). Some passages in the book—including the famous jest about the "pinko-grey" races (PI, 66) and the speech of Aziz about the need of Indians for "kindness, more kindness, and even after that more kindness" (PI, 122)—are absent from the manuscripts; while the latter contain much material that was finally rejected. Forster's admirers are likely to relish many such passages as the account of Fielding's past (MPI, 107–9), that of the chauffeur's origins (MPI, 168), and the rumours of Adela's death: "By four o'clock Adela was dead or dying all over the Civil Station and as far as the Railway. North of the railway she was known to be ill . . . ." (MPI, 395.) They may even be tempted to feel that too many babies have gone out with the bathwater; but in most cases they will probably agree that the interests of economy and form have rightly prevailed.

Some of the changes affect the characterisation perceptibly. Aziz appears to have been observed with almost complete clarity from the outset, but Fielding would have been a subtly different person if he had been allowed to retain his motor-bicycle (MPI, 219), to smoke cigarettes instead of a pipe (MPI, 409; PI, 194), and to practise the characteristic Wilcox ritual of looking at his watch (MPI, 79; cf. HE, 107, 201, 222, 232). Adela (alias Violet, alias Janet, alias Edith) is more aggressive in the earlier manuscript chapters—"she had little self-control and had learnt[12] at Cambridge that one ought to show when one's bored" (MPI, 82)— more like the suffragette *manquée* of the 1960 London stage production. Other examples are noted by Harrison.

Inconsistencies of name are not without significance: at one stage Ronny bore the surname Moore, which, combined with other evidence, suggests that at that period Part III of the novel had not been projected. The numbering and renumbering of

[12] Perhaps from Stewart Ansell.

chapters have already been mentioned, and have their own interest: one most effective change, isolating and emphasising as it does the almost personal power of the climate, is the renumbering of what was originally a single chapter as the present Chapters IX, X, and XI.

Turning to more obvious structural issues, we find in almost every chapter variants of incident: both the engagement and its rupture, for example, are treated very differently in the manuscripts, so is the "bridge party", so is the trial; above all, so is the expedition to the Marabar caves. It is an interesting fact that, of the 101 leaves of MS. B, no less than fifty-five represent earlier drafts of Chapters XIV–XVI, and it is clear that this central episode caused the author an unusual amount of trouble; it seems probable, indeed, that this is one reason why the book was not completed around 1913. (Another may have been the need to refresh his memory of Indian English.) These drafts vary greatly from each other and from the book. In one version (MPI, 310) the famous account of the echo is given in the form of a dialogue, in the first cave, between Aziz and Adela (Edith); in another (MPI, 337–8) the echo is linked with Fielding's reflections, not Mrs. Moore's, and it is Fielding, not Aziz, who finds the field-glasses, while the two men have apparently been acquainted long enough for Aziz to have "compelled" Fielding to learn the four lines of Persian poetry which are quoted in Chapter II (PI, 22) but are not in MS. A at that point. Some of the writing illustrates well the modest beginnings from which so much of the impressive final version emerges: in one early four-leaf draft Adela, in a supposedly hysterical state, is actually made to say something as wooden and unconvincing as "Miss Derek, I have been lacking in sympathy myself all my life, I feel." (MPI, 316.)

This fragment of four leaves is perhaps the most intriguing in the entire trove, for it answers unequivocally the question which, *pace* the confident conclusions of some critics, the author has so scrupulously refrained from answering in the book: whether (ignoring the more implausible explanations) Adela was the victim of hallucination or of attempted assault by somebody other than Aziz. In this early stage of the book's genesis, at least, there *was* an assault (MPI, 315); as is confirmed elsewhere in some working notes headed "Situation at the catastrophe" (MPI, 723). This is one of a number of notes scattered around the versos and margins, of which two others may be mentioned as examples of the light they shed on the author's discarded intentions and his methods: the remarkable "Aziz & Janet drift into one another's arms—then apart" (MPI, 722), and the marginal note against McBryde's appearance in Chapter XVIII, "Introduce him earlier" (MPI, 364)—as is duly done in Chapter V of the book.

Finally the manuscripts shed light on one or two doubtful readings in the published texts. The curious use of "draggled" (PI, 220) in the apparent sense of "tangled", is confirmed (MPI, 464), as is the substantival use of "beat up" (PI, 275; MPI, 588) where "heat up" might have been expected—though this may be one of those slips of the pen to which I have referred. On the other hand, future editions of *A Passage to India* will surely have to correct "Others praised Him without attributes" (PI, 327) to ". . . with attributes" (MPI, 698), "half dead" (PI, 331) to "'half deaf" (MPI, 706), and "fifty five-hundred" (PI, 335; MPI, 716) to the reading from MS. B, "fifty or five-hundred" (MPI, 717).[13]

The paramount interest of the manuscripts, however, is the remarkable light they throw on "the process of creation" and on one of the great English novels; and I cannot end this essay without expressing the hope that other manuscripts of the same author will one day enter the public domain.

[13] For drawing my attention to all these points I am indebted to George H. Thomson. In the last example the actual reading of MS. B. is "50 or 500".

A Forster Miscellany: Thoughts on the Uncollected Writings

by George H. Thomson

"The longer one lives the less one feels to have done, and I am both surprised and glad to discover from this bibliography that I have written so much."

Forster was twenty-one years old in 1900 when he began to write for the periodical press. He continued with such writing for the next sixty-five years, and the *Bibliography* he speaks of, by Miss B. J. Kirkpatrick, identifies 533 contributions to periodicals and newspapers.[1] After seventy-one negligible items, mainly letters, have been subtracted, the meaningful figure is 462. Of these, Forster has reprinted 152: in *The Collected Short Stories* (11), *Pharos and Pharillon* (11), *Abinger Harvest* (62), *Two Cheers for Democracy* (65), *Marianne Thornton* (1), *The Hill of Devi* (1), and *The Longest Journey*, World's Classics edition (1). He has left uncollected 310 contributions, a substantial body of writing comprising something

[1] *A Bibliography of E. M. Forster* (Hart-Davis, London, 1965). The reader will notice that Section C records 516 contributions. The total of 533 mentioned above and all other figures in this essay are based on the second (revised) impression, 1968, the page proofs of which were generously made available by Miss Kirkpatrick and her publishers.

over 300,000 words. At least one third of these stories, essays, reviews, and notes deserve to be rescued and made into a book. Like the pieces already collected, they tend with only a little awkwardness to arrange themselves into subject classes. This is the basis of the following six sections which contain a sampling of the more than a hundred good things Forster has left in obscurity.

I Fiction

It is no favour to an author to gather up and then disburse writings which are best left, on account of their ephemeral nature, to the mercies of oblivion or the scholar. But the general reader has his own legitimate interests. In the case of a famous novelist these interests may justly include ready access to all the writer's fiction: good and bad alike.

In Forster's case the items to be gathered are few. First, "Albergo Empedocle" (1903),[2] not the best and not quite the worst of the early stories, but the only one which remains uncollected. Next, "Arctic Summer [Fragment of an Unfinished Novel]" written in the spring of 1914 and published in *A Tribute to Benjamin Britten on his Fiftieth Birthday* (1963). Attached to the fragment is an analysis of the novelist's difficulties when the story is about a hero who strays into the modern world—a world not congenial to heroes either in fact or fiction. Another fragment (undated and described as the opening chapter) was published in 1948 as "Entrance to an Unwritten Novel". Mrs. March, with her children in tow, is nearing Suez on her return from India to England. As she does so the reader gets interesting glimpses of a group of children playing and quarrelling—an uncommon subject for Forster. The narrative has some good ideas and imaginative touches, but so many characters are introduced in a short space that the action becomes clogged.

The next item promises to be of more substance than these

[2] Details of publication will be found by looking up the year and the title in Section C of Miss Kirkpatrick's *Bibliography*. In the case of entries which appear only in the second impression details are noted in the text.

mere fragments. "Three Courses and Dessert, Being a New and Gastronomic Version of the Old Game of 'Consequences' " (published in *Wine and Food*, 1944) is a bizarre short story set in a hotel cellar where dinner is being served during a wartime air-raid. This brittle social comedy with a grim ending is not easy to follow, not well pointed, not successful. But, like British food in 1944, its composition arouses interest.

Two retrospective glimpses might round off Section I. "A Room without a View", looking back from 1958, tells what happened to the characters in *A Room with a View*. (It is typical that the most memorable statement is about a place: "Windy Corner disappeared, its garden was built over, and the name of Honeychurch resounded in Surrey no more!") "The Old School" (1934) discovers Herbert and Agnes Pembroke, formerly of *The Longest Journey*, confronting a collection of essays with the above title edited by Graham Greene. Most of the writers contributing to the book did not like their schools, which so upsets Herbert that he calls Agnes to the support of his opinions. But even the obtuse Herbert cannot hide it from himself that she is not deeply concerned and not properly attentive. Yet she is, as ever, vocal and decisive. " 'Well, if the boys do not come from proper schools it is naturally not a proper book,' says Agnes, who is adding up the washing under the rim of the study table where she thinks I cannot see it. 'I don't think you ought to worry—(one pound three and two)—over that, Herbert.' " So much for Herbert and Agnes. For Forster it is the last of Sawston.

II   Early writings

Though he has republished well over half his writings from the decade 1903–12, Forster has left untouched two groups of items: a dozen satirical contributions to Cambridge journals, ten of them dating from 1900 to 1901; and a series of papers published in the *Working Men's College Journal*, beginning in 1907.

"On Bicycling" (1900) is a better than average display of Forster's early satirical bent.

Besides children, the Cambridge bicyclist must beware of steep hills. They can indeed be descried at a considerable distance, but are none the less insidious. The C.T.C. have missed this part of England in their paternal survey: as far as I know only one hill near has their sign-board—the Haslingfield. It is short and steep, ending in a low wall, which not unsuitably forms the boundary of a grave yard. The Gog Magogs are unmarked. The precipitous Madingley, however, has gained notoriety. Many years ago, the then Vice-Chancellor used to descend it at a terrific rate, carried by his impetus past the sunny pleasure domes of the observatory right into the scene of his labours. One day the hill rebelled at the insult and threw him off. An enterprising tyre company profited by this to erect a circular caution on the top, but democratic England has not brooked classification with a Vice-Chancellor and the caution has been stoned till it is illegible.

Along with the contrasts and ironies, one notes the animateness of nature and the coming down to earth of one who inclined to defy her laws.

Deflation of a different sort is at work in "A Tragic Interior, 2 (Being a Further Attempt to Assist the Earnest Student of Aeschylus, by Means of an Interpretation of the *Choephori*)". Here the comic idea is to inject the simplest domestic operations into the grandest tragic events. These satiric displays show the undergraduate Forster ready to prick the balloons of pomposity and high seriousness while yet retaining his urbanity.

Of the papers in the *Working Men's College Journal*, one of the most interesting is "Pessimism in Literature" (1907), read on 1 December 1906. It catches Forster in a slightly odd stance. Noting that the great European writers, Ibsen, Zola, and Tolstoy were pessimists, he goes on to emphasise the morbid sadness of contemporary English writing by naming Gissing, Stevenson, Henry James, and Hardy. He accepts it as a fact that marriage (the old answer) is no longer a suitable ending for a book. The only permanence is change, and for the modern writer separation is "the end that really satisfies him—not simply the separation that comes through death, but the more tragic separation of people who part before they need, or part because they have seen each other too closely. Here is something that does last. . . ." *The Wings of the Dove* is his illustration.

Having got this far, Forster makes an extremely interesting admission (possibly it should be called a calculation): "The truth is that modern art has not succeeded in depicting all modern life." The spirit of the age determines what the author can present as permanent; it determines the emphasis on sadness. Though the author as a man may look for what is cheerful, and noble, and gracious, this cannot now be the dominant note of his art.

It is a little odd, but not on that account improbable, to see Forster thus dictated to. For it may well be that he was impelled to put aside *A Room with a View*, a story requiring a happily-ever-after ending, precisely because he did not yet have the courage to defy this spirit of the age. He ends his paper with these words: "I uphold optimism in life. I do not uphold optimism in literature. . . . I am as anxious as anyone for cheerful books; but they must be cheerful with sincerity." "Cheerful with sincerity" does not adequately characterise Forster's novels and stories, for he had his own forms of separation to undercut the cheer. But he was incapable of that sustained morbid sadness dictated by the spirit of pessimism—as even *The Longest Journey* testifies. What the article shows is Forster askew with his age without his being fully aware of the angle of his stance.

III   *India and Egypt*

Forster lived and worked and travelled in India and Egypt during five of the first twenty-five years of his adult life. This experience is justly reflected in his publications. Four of his books as well as a substantial number of essays in *Abinger Harvest* are about these countries. A few items of exceptional interest are still uncollected.

One, called "The Gods of India" (1914), reviews a work of that title by E. O. Martin. Forster may have left it buried because it is finally a devastating critique of the reverend gentleman's book. Today its principal interest is the light it throws on *A Passage to India*. With great clarity it distinguishes the Eastern from the

Western view of religion. "And the promise is not that a man shall see God, but that he shall be God. He is God already, but imperfectly grasps the mystery. He will realise the universe as soon as he realises himself, and pity, courage, reliability, etc., may help him or may hinder him in his quest; it depends. The deities may help him, or they may mislead, like the shows of earth; it depends, depends on the step he has taken just before." It is in this sense that the India of Forster's novel is after all a mystery, not a muddle.

Two remarkable articles relate to the Indian temple. The first, "The Temple" (1919), is an ironic review of annual archaeological reports. Forster is on the side of the temple. He has a profoundly intuitive grasp of its meaning: "When we tire of being pleased and of being improved, and of the other gymnastics of the West, and care, or think we care, for Truth alone; then the Indian Temple exerts its power, and beckons down absurd or detestable vistas to an exit unknown to the Parthenon." It is well to remember these words as one reads Forster's confession in "The Individual and his God" (1940) that until now he had not known the symbolism of the temple: the outside, the world mountain; the inside, the isolated shrine of the individual alone with his God. The deep appeal of the meaning discovered in 1940 echoes his earlier awareness of the temple as opening on to a truth unknown to the orderly and community-spirited West.

A Hindu temple, which characteristically is not a temple but a palace, plays an essential role in *The Hill of Devi*. There in the temple-palace the festival of Gokul Ashtami takes place during August 1921. Forster's letters "describe (if too facetiously) rites in which an European can seldom have shared" (HD, 100). *A Passage to India*, published in 1924, describes the same rites, yet the outlook is now radically transformed. Other instances of this process show it is not art alone but art touched by the wisdom of time and perspective that induces such change. For example, in *The Hill of Devi* Forster writes, shortly after arriving at the residence of His Highness: "The New Palace . . . is still building, and the parts of it that were built ten years ago are already falling

down. You would weep at the destruction, expense, and hideous-
ness, and I do almost. We live amongst rubble and mortar, and
excavations whence six men carry a basket of earth, no larger
than a cat's, twenty yards once in five minutes." (HD, 59.) As his
stay at the New Palace lengthened he grew more and more
philosophical and sympathetic. But complete acceptance only
comes much later, in an admirable essay called "Woodlanders on
Devi" (1939).

> Eighteen years ago, in a palace in India, I read Hardy's *Wood-
> landers*. The palace was in course of construction. Three sides of
> the quadrangle were under the Office of Works, the fourth side,
> which was semi-sacred, was under the Commander-in-Chief. He
> was a simple, affable officer, who did not trouble himself with his
> army; indeed how could he, when they had no uniforms? His
> main duties were social: he drank port with us, he joined in a
> card-game called Jubbu, sitting on a carpet in the quadrangle
> while the coolies clanged and the dust fell and the cards were
> dealt anti-clockwise with the happiest results. He was full of little
> courtesies, and drove up one evening clasping a live fish in a
> towel; he hoped it would do for my supper. Rooted in reality, he
> did not trouble himself with the building; his side of the quad-
> rangle rose but slowly, and never reached the stage of having
> floors. This did not signify, since it was intended as a memorial
> to the late Maharajah, rather than for residence; a few workmen
> hit at it, and contended with the superior hordes of the Office of
> Works, and saved his honour.

"There are a hundred Indias, but only two or three Egypts."
So begins "Two Egypts" (1919), an often funny review filled
with irony and interest. "Gippo English" (1917) is equally funny
and more touching, as it commemorates the early years of the war
when the English of the Egyptians

> . . . was in the full innocence and exuberance of a polyglot
> youth. It feared nothing, it attempted all things both in prose and
> rhyme, and Arab and Syrian and Greek sang hymns of welcome
> together like the morning stars. Not realising how youth flies, I
> never copied those inscriptions down. The loss is irreparable for

that primitive insouciance will never return. Take for instance the following lyric outburst—it served as sign-board to a Restaurant: —"Have you first-class meals of Breakfast for Lunch Tea and Supper." Or again:—"Here is Alexandre's garden where Australian heroes eat and shoot" . . . and if you wanted to be shaved there was "Antiseptic Red Cross civility and cleanliness" and if you wanted to buy something there was a shop succinctly entitled "Ten Tousend Things".

The most deeply impressive of Forster's uncollected Egyptian articles is "A Birth in the Desert" (1924).

> On the fringe of the Libyan Desert, forty miles west from Alexandria and two miles south of the sea, some remarkable buildings are standing . . . puzzling buildings, abrupt, visible for miles, yet spiritually at home. Who built them? The guide-book does not say. What is their date? What style are they in? Egyptian? Not exactly, but then we are not exactly in Egypt; Egypt starts with the irrigation a few miles behind; Egypt was the river Nile. Are they Tunisian, Algerian, southern Spanish? Not exactly, again. Did the Bedouins put them up? Impossible, Bedouins don't build, they are nomads; look at their tents there, almost Mongolian in outline, and harmonising with the low ridges of the hills. Then whence came this austere beautiful town, with its unfinished walls, solemn market-place, court-house, antique memorial column? . . . Our last conjecture was, indeed, the nearest to the truth. Bedouins don't build. But if they did, they would build like this. Something has evidently happened, some influence has passed over the desert, and the latent architectural capabilities of a race have been stirred.

Burg el Arab only dates from 1918. It was built for the Bedouins not as a home but as a spiritual and trading centre. Now that the English have left Egypt, its fate is in doubt. That is the subject of the article. But the significance is that Burg el Arab took form in 1918: "It is one of the few creations of an epoch that gloried in degradation and destruction; one of the few proofs then forthcoming that the life of man, like the life of plants, refused to lie buried in ugliness and muddle for ever."

IV   *History, society, and the arts*

This section is a catch-all, but important. By analogy with Section III it might be called *England and Europe* were it not that the entire planet is included in "A Great History" (1920), a long review of the first volume of H. G. Wells's *Outline of History*. In a commentary notable for its ambivalence Forster calls it "a great book; a possession for ever, for the ever of one's tiny life". He praises its arrangement, its selection and its style. Arrangement is a great quality, but a negative one: "it is the faculty of not muddling the reader, and Wells possesses it to a high degree." Next: "There is not a man alive who could have selected from those millions of years so well, and we had better acknowledge this handsomely, and give the writer 'good' again." Finally, style: "The surface of Wells' English is poor, and he does not improve its effect when he tints it purple. But it does do its job. . . ."

In turning from "merits" to "defects", Forster points to Wells's one irreparable weakness, his lack of imagination. His great historical figures do not live. "It is a history of movements, not of man." Worse, Wells "confuses information with wisdom, like most scientists. . . ." As the review proceeds the difference in outlook separating the two men grows to an abyss. Forster admits that "it is only an optimist who could attempt a history of this planet. To the rest of us it is a planetful of scraps, many of which are noble and beautiful, but there seems not any proof that it progresses." He concludes: "Men want to alter this planet, yet also believe that it is not worth altering and that behind it is something unalterable, and their perfect historian will be he who enters with equal sympathy into these contradictory desires." Is such a historian possible? Is he likely, so caught up in his double vision, to have the staying power for a history not of an age or of an empire but of a planet? Forster does not say. Rather he advises the reader to buy Wells's *Outline*. But one feels—at least at this distance of time—it might be better just to do without such a history.

About another history book, Hilaire Belloc's *Europe and the Faith*, Forster shows no ambivalence. His review, called "A

Cautionary Tale" (1920), is a well-mannered but biting exposé: "In his introduction Mr. Belloc states his qualifications for writing a book about Europe. They are even more dramatic than one expected, for the chief of them is Intuition. In a deep and mystic sense, he is one with his subject-matter, and for this reason: because he is a member of the Roman Catholic Church. As a Catholic he has 'conscience', 'con-scientia', that intimate knowledge of Europe through identity that is denied to Protestants, Agnostics, Japanese, and Jews. 'The Faith is Europe and Europe is the Faith.' " Forster, though much disadvantaged by his lack of Faith, proceeds to an outline of the book's argument. After that, having noticed the author's intention to persuade, coerce, and deceive the reader, he sets out to pick apart the snares, traps and tricks employed to that end. He concludes: "The devices are rather inherent in Mr. Belloc's own character. He would have been just as slippery as an Agnostic or a Protestant."

"A Popular Theatre" (1919) shifts the scene to society and the arts:

> Dramatically, a theatre may range the whole of life, but in its architecture it is rigidly genteel. The buildings in which we witness *Strife* or *Ghosts* or *L'annonce faite à Marie* descend from the theatres of German petty courts, and recall that elegant ancestry in their arrangements—boxes for the nobility and plutocracy, a "royal" box where specimens of that class can be mounted on exhibit, stalls and dress circle for the bourgeoisie, cramped back seats for the poor, where they are huddled away like servants, unable to see through the bodies of the rich and often unable to hear through their chatter. No generous mind can admire such an arrangement. It is unfair to the poor and bad for the play. The playwright may be opening heaven or overturning earth on his side of the curtain, but the audience on theirs are wedged into the framework of a snobby social system, and their position reacts on his.

So begins a review of two books by Romain Rolland—a loosely organised essay, but one that is full of interest. Here, for instance, is Rolland, with Forster's full approval, damning the State: "By its very definition the State belongs to the past. No matter how new the forms of life it represents, it arrests and congeals them. It is its function to petrify everything with which it comes into contact, and turn living into bureaucratic ideals."

Such a rooted distrust of man-made order and bureaucratic formalism contributes to Forster's passionate distaste for censorship. Articles in which he speaks out well about this are "The New Censorship" (1928) concerning the suppression of Radclyffe Hall's novel *The Well of Loneliness*, and "Mr. D. H. Lawrence and Lord Brentford" (1930), an informative review of Lawrence's *Pornography and Obscenity* and Brentford's *Do We Need a Censor?* He ends with a plea for tolerance.

Forster's wish to bring into single focus his sympathy for ordinary humanity and his distrust of state bureaucracy leads unavoidably to his difficulty over Communism. The best-known expression of this difficulty is his speech to the International Congress of Writers at Paris in June 1935 : "And you may have guessed that I am not a Communist, though perhaps I might be one if I was a younger and a braver man, for in Communism I can see hope. It does many things which I think evil, but I know that it intends good." This statement should be supplemented with "The Long Run" (1938), a review of Christopher Caudwell's *Studies in a Dying Culture*.

"Liberty is a leaky word, and it is surprising that Communists should venture on board of it." But to their credit they do, says Forster. They begin by attacking the bourgeois idea of personal freedom, go on to define the Communist ideal of freedom through social co-operation, then advance to the dictatorship of the proletariat which will somehow some day wither "and Karl Marx will turn into Father Christmas". The result:

> Just as we reach the summit of the exposition, and, our bourgeois illusions demolished, are expecting a positive goal, the exposition collapses. This collapse occurs in all religions—first the careful reasoning, the analysis of existing ills, and then the desperate jump to glory. Communism, like Christianity, jumps. And the shock is the bigger because of its previous aridity, its harsh technical arguments, economic and psychological, its

contempt for all that is pleasant, wayward and soft. On we move, through the dictatorship of the proletariat to the full consciousness of the causality of society—and then we get a surprise-stocking. We open it: to discover that liberty means doing what is best for everybody else.

The variety of Forster's writing may be seen in two pieces satiric and comic, arising from World Wars I and II. "The Sitters" (1920) is a review of *Adventures in Interviewing* by Isaac Marcosson, a man who contrived to introduce himself into the private apartments of many of the great ones of his day. Forster writes:

> But as he himself points out it is a miracle that could not have happened in normal times. His success is due to that painful yet apposite catastrophe of a European war. . . . Without an interviewer great people scarcely exist. He creates the necessary bustle round them and thus dissipates the sense of *ennui* that too often creeps over the public when fighting has continued for three years; he reminds us that great men are on high, communicating with each other over our heads. He tells us the little things they say. For instance, Lord Haig said, "It is a war of youth," and he he said it "not without sadness"; it was "a flash of that tender inner thing which strong men so often hide behind a grim or stern exterior", but from Mr. Marcosson it was not hidden. It is quite overwhelming when a great man has an ordinary decent emotion like this. One scarcely knows which way to look.

"You Sausage" (1941), though a product of the restricted rations of World War II, transcends its origins.

YOU SAUSAGE!

Hurled across the school playground at me, half a century ago, these words used to leave my heart in equilibrium. They could have been better but they might have been worse. They might have been "You Stinkpot!" To be called a sausage was not an irreparable social disaster for a little boy, and sometimes, by assuming a jollity which I was far from feeling, I succeeded in diverting my persecutors to some other target. "They do not really like me," I thought, "still they are not quite sure about me."

Which, you sausage, is exactly what I feel about you today. I do not really like you, still I am not quite sure about you. You could have been better, but you might have been a Lunch-Roll! You have possibilities for good which you do not always neglect. The French, with their notorious voluptuousness, have realised this, and one of the few sentences in their language which I have mastered runs "Si ces saucissons sont bons, donne-moi un." So French! Alertness, caution, discrimination, resignation and greed all find their places in that subtle cadence. If these sausages are good (but not otherwise) give me one. Give other people bad ones. I reserve my verdict.

V Literature

Forster, like many writers of this century, has practised the art of book-reviewing. He began seriously to do this in 1914 and continued until 1961. During all this time his output has, with one exception, maintained a modest average of three reviews a year, though the actual number has varied from zero to thirteen. The exception is the period 1919–20 during which his production soared to the startling total of sixty-eight. This single flurry of activity in combination with a steady accretion over the years has resulted in 207 book reviews plus eleven theatre reviews. These comprise nearly one-half of Forster's 462 significant contributions to newspapers and periodicals. Yet from his first review in 1906 (*Some Literary Eccentrics* by John Fyvie) to his last in 1961 (*Growing* by Leonard Woolf), he has selected only thirty-six for republication. Contrast with this the fate of 244 non-reviews—stories, articles, talks, notes—which for convenience will be called essays. Of these, 116 have been republished. Even among the more than a hundred reviews of strictly literary books—novels, plays, and poems; memoirs and letters by creative writers; and works of literary criticism—even here three out of every four items are uncollected. And among the non-literary reviews, including theatre, the neglected proportion rises to a startling nine out of ten.

Essays and talks will more often be of permanent interest than reviews arising from the occasion of a book's first publication. But it may seem surprising that the disproportion is so great: nearly one in two of the essays republished as against only one in six of the reviews. Here Forster's discriminations may be put to the test by scrutinising what he excluded. An evaluation of the 310 uncollected items confirms his judgement: nearly half the ungathered essays merit republication, but less than one-third of the non-literary reviews and less than one-quarter of the literary reviews are similarly deserving. Thus the body of literary material which swam into view on a first glance at Miss Kirkpatrick's *Bibliography* has proved on closer inspection to have more size than substance.

In a symposium on the theme "Reviewing Reviewed" (The *Author*, LIII, Summer 1943, 67–8) Forster set out his principles. Older reviewers should be careful in their handing out of blame. Younger ones may treat their elders, also their contemporaries, with more freedom, even with irresponsibility if they like. This will keep literature from being stifled. By way of example he mentions a "dressing-down" he once gave "pompous old Sir Sydney Lee". His review, still worth reading, of Lee's *King Edward VII: A Biography*, vol. 1 (1925) begins: "This book is dead." Not because the author is stupid or uncritical, says Forster, but because "officialism has destroyed his scale of values."

Another kind of dressing-down was administered in "Well, Well!" (1920). "Anyone who has himself tried to write brightly yet thoughtfully for the newspapers will read these republished articles of Mr. Chesterton's with a peculiar gloom. This is what bright thoughts look like when in book form!" And the conclusion: "It's saddening, and the sadness increases when one reflects that one's no better oneself, and far less talented. If Mr. Chesterton's articles are worthless, so is this article that deals with them. Let the lover of literature throw all of them together into his waste-paper basket, and forget that such things could be." Well, well! One reader admits to having read this article several times, always with pleasure.

Forster's first review of a serious novel, though published in the

Daily News and Leader, is far from newspaper-bright. Its date is 1915, its length approximately 1,300 words, its subject Virginia Woolf's *The Voyage Out*. The review is of great interest in showing the relations of these two Bloomsbury writers. At this date Forster is thirty-six and has published four novels and a dozen short stories; Mrs. Woolf is thirty-three and here offers her first novel. Forster has deep respect for her education, her intellect, and her art.

> Few women writers are educated. A gentleman ought not to say such a thing, but it is, unfortunately, true. Our Queens of the Pen are learned, sensitive, thoughtful even, but they are uneducated, they have never admitted the brain to the heart, much less let it roam over the body. They live in pieces, and their work, when it does live, lives similarly, devoid of all unity save what is imposed by a plot. Here at last is a book which attains unity as surely as *Wuthering Heights*, . . . a book which, while written by a woman . . . soars straight out of local questionings into the intellectual day.

In this opening part of his analysis, which includes some remarks about Mrs. Woolf's characterisation not being vivid, Forster moves with his usual assurance. But for the rest of the review he is feeling his way, looking out for qualities he can respond to, exploring, so it seems, the differences between his own fictional world and hers, and the result is a curious blending of Mr. Forster and Mrs. Woolf. The blending in one passage becomes so alchemical that it engenders a quality touching both of them yet belonging to neither.

> If the above criticism is correct, if Mrs. Woolf does not "do" her four main characters very vividly, and is apt to let them all become clever together, and differ only by their opinions, then on what does her success depend? . . . She believes in adventure—here is the main point—believes in it passionately, and knows that it can only be undertaken alone. Human relations are no substitute for adventure, because when real they are uncomfortable, and when comfortable they must be unreal. It is for a voyage into solitude that man was created, and Rachel, Helen, Hewet, Hirst,

all learn this lesson, which is exquisitely reinforced by the setting of tropical scenery—the soul, like the body, voyages at her own risk.

This early comment on Virginia Woolf is symbolic of the fact that as a reviewer of literature Forster has most to say in treating books by and about novelists, and especially the great modern novelists. Among ungathered items, there is his very honest discussion of *What, Then, Must We Do?* ("Poverty's Challenge: The Terrible Tolstoy", 1925) which reveals his attitude to property and poverty, and his perceptive look at Middleton Murry's *Son of Woman: The Story of D. H. Lawrence* in "The Cult of D. H. Lawrence" (1931). And, of course, there is no escaping "The Book of the Age? James Joyce's *Ulysses*" (1926), the often-quoted review which finds the novel brilliant in technique, narrow in its treatment of human nature, and dedicated to spattering the universe with dirt. As for its difficulty: "Even the police are said not to comprehend it fully. . . ." To illustrate Joyce's obscurity and skill, Forster chooses from the Library episode that bit of poetry and dialogue about Shakespeare's second-best bed. Then he explicates the text so well that Joyce comes off better than his critic intended. Though seldom referred to, this is the best part of Forster's discussion.

To it should be added "The Censor Again?" (*The Author*, XLIV, Spring 1934, 78-9), a moderate and careful statement directed to the Society of Authors: *Ulysses* is likely to be published soon in England; it will be most helpful if authors speak up now on its behalf, rather than waiting until the novel is haled into court. "It is a serious book, a difficult book, a depressing book. . . . It is a mirror of the twentieth century's unrest. . . . It is also an amazing assemblage of literary devices, into which no writer can look without finding some salutary caricature of his own method. And it is, possibly, a masterpiece."

Since his last collection of essays in 1951, Forster has published some general articles and talks about well-known writers. To these may be added a very few earlier items. The most memorable is "William Cowper, An Englishman" (1932) on the occasion of the bicentenary of Cowper's birth. Forster ends: "He belongs to the unadvertised, the unorganised, the unscheduled. He has no part in the enormous structure of steel girders and trade upon which Great Britain, like all other Powers, will have to base her culture in the future. That is why his bicentenary fell flat." The best part of the essay is about Cowper's feeling for things English. He loved what he knew, Forster says, "he felt steadily about familiar objects, and they have in his work something of the permanence they get in a sitting-room or in the kitchen garden."

> Consequently, to read him is really to be in England, and the very triteness of his moralising keeps us planted there. Brilliant descriptions and profound thoughts entail disadvantages when they are applied to scenery; they act too much as spot lights; they break the landscape up; they drill through it and come out at the antipodes; they focus too much upon what lies exactly in front. Cowper never does this. He knows that the country doesn't lie in front of us but all around. In front is an elm tree, but behind our backs there is probably another elm tree, and out of the corner of each eye we can see blurs that may represent a third elm and a fourth. And so with the country people, the ploughman or the postman, we may or may not meet them on our walk, but in either case they were somewhere. All this comes out in his work, and we get from it the conviction that we have a humble and inalienable heritage, country England, which no one covets, and which nothing can take away.

A heritage of a different kind is described in "The Legacy of Samuel Butler" (1952), a radio talk about Butler's reputation since 1900, his impact on Forster, and his present standing. "If Butler had not lived, many of us would now be a little deader than we are, a little less aware of the tricks and traps in life, and of our own obtuseness."

A more domestic legacy confronts the reader in "The Charm and Strength of Mrs. Gaskell" (1957). Forster introduces his warm appraisal of her work and especially of her last novel, *Wives and Daughters*, by giving an account of how he met Mrs. Gaskell's daughter. This is a reminder—the comment on Butler is another—

that these essays are personal and, at moments, autobiographical. There is no sharp line dividing them from the group that follows.

VI *Autobiography*

For the novelist autobiography may be creative or reminiscent. Forster has spoken amusingly of the creative variety in "Writers at Bay" (1932). Within the harried ranks of authorship the novelist is peculiarly vulnerable, for he is open to that most treacherous of questions: "Do you put real people into your books?" Say "No" and lie, that is the best policy. For look at the fix Dickens gets himself into over Harold Skimpole. After Leigh Hunt's death Dickens tries to tell the truth:

> He admits that he did "yield too much to the temptation of making Skimpole speak like his old friend", did borrow Hunt's "gay and ostentatious wilfulness", but there the parallel ended. He would have us think that Skimpole consists of a slab of Hunt and slabs of unpleasing and unknown origin. What he does not see, or will not say, is that the matter cannot be argued out, because the fusion between the slabs took place when he was in the creative state. And a man in that state is very ruthless and will make the cruellest discoveries and statements about a friend.

Both the private life of the writer and the public life as it impinges on the private enter the creative stream of the fiction. And both may be subject to the cruellest discoveries.

"Recollectionism" (1937) makes clear that no such rigour pertains to the reminiscent variety of self-portraiture:

> This is an age of autobiographies and recollections, indeed, I don't suppose that the human memory can ever before have been so remorselessly called into print and so gallantly responded. That bishops, burglars and butlers should publish their pasts seems proper enough; for professional reasons they have had much to conceal, and so they should have much to say. That creative artists should be equally chatty surprises me. They might be expected to have said what they wanted to say in their works, and, in the deepest sense, to have drained themselves dry. Still, recollect they do, and frequently to our delight.

A three-decker self-portrait from the pen of E. M. Forster is, on this view of things, unlikely. Which is not to say access to the private is necessarily cut off. One gets the strong impression in reading Forster that two doorways to the personal past are at all times ajar: the two ways of humour and deep attachment. The humour does not open on to a landscape of inner fact—unless the thoughts about "My Wood" or about the Royal Academy pictures in "Me, Them and You" qualify as such, or unless the confessing to one's favourite limerick is an inner fact:

> There was an old lady of Sheen
> Whose musical sense was not keen;
> She said, "It's so odd
> I can never tell God
> Save the Weasel from Pop goes the Queen."
> ("Escaping the House of Common-sense", 1926)

No, the humour appears to open on to some continuing, some unalterable quality, at once personal and impersonal, some inner perspective which is never out of sight for long in either the essays or the fiction. Words are not easily found to describe this combination of laughter and wit, of self-consciousness and sophistication. It is a combination which, offering little in the way of facts, is yet essential to Forster's self-portrait.

The private life revealed through the door opened by deep attachment is much plainer to the view. Here from "Recollectionism" (1937) is a variation on the theme "Love of Wiltshire", a theme which Forster in recent years has treated more circumstantially, but not more movingly: "Wiltshire today—scarred, militarised, droning, screaming—how best can I sink through its ruins thirty years downwards into Figsbury Rings above the Winterbourne, where Wiltshire seemed indestructible and eternal?" And on the human side there are the tributes, arising out of gratitude or affection, into which Forster has unhesitatingly admitted the personal facts needed to explain his appreciation. The most substantial of these is the biography of Lowes Dickinson.

The ways of humour and attachment are at the heart of Forster's

personal style as essayist and novelist. In addition, he has in more
recent years admitted subject-matter which is personal in the
recollectionist manner. He has permitted himself what might be
called Notes towards an Autobiography. These make their first
collected appearance in "Places", the last section of *Two Cheers
for Democracy*. They extend in time from "Clouds Hill" (1938) to
"Mount Lebanon" (1951) and in space from Pretoria to India to
the United States. Since 1951 they have been joined by other
Notes: *Marianne Thornton, The Hill of Devi*, a personal introduction
to *The Longest Journey*, the well-known "Indian Entries" (1962)
in *Encounter*, and a variety of articles and talks, a few of which are
wholly autobiographical. Two of the latter are outstanding:
"Recollections of Nassenheide" (1959) for its liveliness and the
evocative power of its language, and "A Presidential Address to
the Cambridge Humanists—Summer 1959" (1963) for the interest
of its subject.

Nassenheide was the German home of the Countess von Arnim,
better known as "Elizabeth", the author of the once-famous
Elizabeth and her German Garden. Forster was engaged in 1905 as a
part of the teaching staff and it is the four members of this staff,
himself included, whom he describes. But parallel to the human
interest another theme appears, reappears, persists. It is the German countryside. "You cannot imagine the radiance that descended upon that flat iron-coloured land in May." Forster returns
at the end of the essay to this experience:

> It is curious that Germany, a country which I do not know well
> or instinctively embrace, should twice have seduced me through
> her countryside. I have described the first occasion. The second
> was half a century later when I stayed in a remote hamlet in
> Franconia. The scenery was more scenic than in Pomerania.
> There were swelling green hills rising into woodlands. There
> were picturesque castles and distant views. But the two districts
> resembled each other in their vastness and openness and in their
> freedom from industrialism. They were free from smoke and
> wires, and masts and placards, and they were full of living air:
> they remind me of what our own countryside used to be before
> it was ruined.

"A Presidential Address" takes as its text: How I lost my faith. Like any good confession or sermon—there's a bit of both here—it can accommodate personal digressions and impersonal *exempla*. One such digression expands to the proportions of a major theme: The speaker is unsympathetic towards Christ. The compassion may be eloquent but the preachy élitism, the absence of fun, and the lack of intellectual power chill Forster's blood. In his youth he did not find Christ a "satisfactory father-figure, brother-figure, friend, what you will". The next paragraph exposes, unconsciously it would seem, at least one of the reasons for this failure. "I may add that my indifference towards Christ did not prevent me from usurping his position myself in my childish daydream. All I had to do was to walk about the countryside while my disciples followed me. They listened. I talked. I liked that." Men will reveal horrendous acts and ghastly facts, but never the innermost secrets of their daydreams. It is a startling instance of Forster's honesty that he should tell his daydream, and in this place where he is, through its hidden implications, saying to the reader: I so easily identified myself in childish fancy with Christ that he did not in my grown-up view seem a satisfactory father- or brother-figure.

Forster's main theme is how he lost his faith slowly, quietly, unspectacularly. To adapt still further the famous local phrase: the defusing of Christianity was effected with comparatively little fuss. For one thing, he "never had much sense of sin". For another, just mentioned, his response to Christ was negative. At the end of his speech, after the digressions and *exempla* have enriched the theme, Forster returns for the last time to his unadventurous loss.

> Maybe I have softened my loss of faith retrospectively, and underwent crises and tumults which my subconscious has suppressed. Or maybe a Humanism which has been gained so softly may not stand by me in the hour of death. I should be glad if it did. I do not want to recant and muddle people. But I do not take the hour of death too seriously. It may scare, it may hurt, it probably ends the individual, but in comparison to the hours when a man is alive, the hour of death is almost negligible.

Bibliography

Miss B. J. Kirkpatrick's admirable *A Bibliography of E. M. Forster* (Hart-Davis, London, 1965; second, revised impression 1968) makes it unnecessary to do more than list Forster's books (and one or two pamphlets), referring the reader to her work for details of the various editions:

NOVELS
1905 *Where Angels Fear to Tread*
1907 *The Longest Journey*
1908 *A Room with a View*
1910 *Howards End*
1924 *A Passage to India*

SHORT STORIES
1911 *The Celestial Omnibus and Other Stories*
1928 *The Eternal Moment and Other Stories*
(These two volumes form what in various editions are called the *Collected Short Stories, Collected Stories* and *Collected Tales*)

GUIDEBOOK
1922 *Alexandria: A History and a Guide*

ESSAYS
1923 *Pharos and Pharillon* (on Egyptian topics)
1936 *Abinger Harvest*
1951 *Two Cheers for Democracy*

CRITICISM
1927 *Aspects of the Novel*

BIOGRAPHY
1934 *Goldsworthy Lowes Dickinson*
1956 *Marianne Thornton*

PAGEANT PLAYS
1934 *Pageant of Abinger* (included in some editions of *Abinger Harvest*)
1940 *England's Pleasant Land*

OPERA LIBRETTO
1951 *Billy Budd* (with Eric Crozier; music by Benjamin Britten)

LETTERS
1953 *The Hill of Devi* (India, 1912–13 and 1921)

Selection from the rapidly growing list of books and essays on Forster becomes ever more invidious, and will not be attempted here. The reader is referred instead to "E. M. Forster: An Annotated Checklist of Writings about Him", compiled and edited by Helmut E. Gerber, in *English Fiction in Transition (1880–1920)*, Spring 1959, vol. II, leaves 4–27, published by the English Department, Purdue University, West Lafayette, Indiana, and to "Criticism of E. M. Forster: A Selected Checklist", by Maurice Beebe and Joseph Brogunier, in *Modern Fiction Studies*, 1961, vol. VII, pp. 284–92. Gerber's checklist is being kept up to date in later volumes of *English Fiction in Transition*, now entitled *English Literature in Transition*.

The Contributors

ELIZABETH BOWEN, who is Irish, published her first book, *Encounters*, a volume of short stories, in 1923. Her latest novel, *Eva Trout*, appeared in January 1969. Her best-known works are, probably, *The House in Paris* (1935), *The Death of the Heart* (1938), *The Heat of the Day* (1949) and *The Little Girls* (1964). She has also written some non-fiction: *Bowen's Court* (1942), *The Shelbourne* (1951), and *A Time in Rome* (1960).

PATRICK WILKINSON, born in 1907, entered King's College, Cambridge, from Charterhouse in 1926, and has remained there as Fellow, Lecturer in Classics, and for various periods Dean, Senior Tutor, and Vice-Provost. He is also Orator of the University and Reader in Latin Literature, on which he has written a number of books. He compiled, with R. H. Bulmer, the *King's College Register 1919–1958*. From 1945 to 1952 he and his wife provided Forster with rooms in their house.

DAVID GARNETT, born in 1892, is the son of Edward Garnett the critic and Constance Garnett the translator of Russian literature. After the 1914–18 war, in which he was a conscientious objector, he started a bookshop with Francis Birrell, but gave it up after the success of *Lady into Fox* and *A Man in the Zoo.* He married first Ray Marshall (died 1940) and second Angelica Bell, daughter of Clive and Vanessa Bell. He has also been a publisher and a farmer, and is a Fellow of Imperial College and a C.B.E. He has written some twenty novels and edited the letters of T. E. Lawrence and the novels of T. L. Peacock.

K. NATWAR-SINGH, who was born in 1931, earned first-class honours in History from St. Stephen's College, Delhi. Later he attended Corpus Christi College, Cambridge, and it was at Cambridge that he met Forster. In 1953 he joined the Indian Foreign Service and has since been assigned to Peking and to New York, with India's Permanent Mission to the U.N. He is now Director in Prime Minister Indira Gandhi's Secretariat in New Delhi. His publications include: *E. M. Forster: A Tribute* (1964), *The Legacy of Nehru* (1965), and *Tales from Modern India* (1966).

SIR ALEC RANDALL, born in 1892, studied at University College London and Tübingen University. After working in the Foreign Office and Ministry of Information during the First World War, he served in the regular British Diplomatic Service and the Foreign Office from 1920 until his retirement, as British Ambassador in Copenhagen, in 1953. He was knighted in 1949. His writings include numerous reviews, in various English and American periodicals, of contemporary German literature, and two books, *Vatican Assignment* (1956) and *Discovering Rome* (1960).

WILLIAM ROERICK'S name appears in the dedication of *Two Cheers for Democracy.* A graduate of Hamilton College, he has appeared on the Broadway stage in John Gielgud's *Hamlet,* Katharine Cornell's *Saint Joan, The Burning Glass, The Right*

Honorable Gentleman, Marat/de Sade, and Harold Pinter's *The Home-coming.* With Thomas Coley he has written for television. Their Broadway play, *The Happiest Years,* starred Peggy Wood. They have recently dramatised Storm Jameson's novel, *A Month Soon Goes.*

W. J. H. SPROTT, whose name also appears in the dedication of *Two Cheers for Democracy,* is Emeritus Professor of Psychology at the University of Nottingham. A graduate of the University of Cambridge, he went to the University College, Nottingham, in 1925 as Lecturer in Psychology. He was appointed Professor of Philosophy in 1948, and Professor of Psychology in 1960. As Public Orator he presented E. M. Forster for an Honorary Degree in 1951. His books include *Sociology* (1949), *Social Psychology* (1952) and *Human Groups* (1958).

BENJAMIN BRITTEN, O.M., C.H., is the composer of more than a dozen operas—for one, *Billy Budd,* E. M. Forster was a co-librettist—and of numerous other works, of which the *War Requiem* is perhaps the most famous. He is also a pianist who has accompanied Peter Pears in many recitals, an occasional conductor, director of the English Opera Group, and an artistic director of the Aldeburgh Festival, which he helped to found in 1948. He is a Freeman of the Boroughs of Aldeburgh, where he lives, and of Lowestoft, where he was born fifty-five years ago.

JOHN ARLOTT, who was born in 1914, has been a clerk in a mental hospital, a police detective, and a B.B.C. producer, and is now a writer, a topographer, and a broadcaster who is particularly well known for his cricket commentaries. He has twice stood as a Liberal candidate for Epping, and has published two volumes of poems, two anthologies of poetry, and books on cricket, cheese, and places.

B. W. FAGAN, born in 1893, was a scholar of Rugby School and of Queen's College, Oxford. After taking a first class in Classical Mods in 1913, he was saved from Greats by the First World War, in which he served till wounded and discharged in 1918. In 1919 he was employed by Edward Arnold as educational editor, was taken into partnership in 1921, and succeeded the founder as Chairman from 1931 till his retirement in 1960; over those three decades he saw Forster's books through the press. He served on the Council of the Publishers Association for fifteen years and was President in 1945–7.

WILLIAM PLOMER'S best-known writings are the novels *Turbott Wolfe* (1926) and *Museum Pieces* (1952), two autobiographical books, *Double Lives* (1943) and *At Home* (1958), and his *Collected Poems* (1960). He is the editor of Kilvert's *Diary*, and has written the librettos of four operas by Britten. He was the friend "in a younger generation" who first urged Forster to compile *Abinger Harvest*, and to whom in particular it is dedicated. He has only had the privilege of Forster's acquaintance for four-ninths of the novelist's life, but hopes in ten years' time to be able to amend this fraction to one-half.

WILFRED STONE, born in 1917, is Professor of English at Stanford University and the author of *The Cave and the Mountain: A Study of E. M. Forster*, which won the Christian Gauss (Phi Beta Kappa) Prize for literary criticism in 1967. He has also written *Religion and Art of William Hale White ("Mark Rutherford")*, a critical biography (1954), as well as numerous articles on literature, education and civil rights. He has co-authored two textbooks, the later of which is *Prose Style: A Handbook for Writers* (1968).

MALCOLM BRADBURY is a literary critic and novelist, and Senior Lecturer in English and American Literature at the University of East Anglia. He has written a critical study of Evelyn Waugh (1964), and edited and contributed to *E. M. Forster: A Collection of Critical Essays* (1966). His novels are *Eating People Is Wrong* (1959) and *Stepping Westward* (1965). He is also co-author of two stage revues for the Birmingham Repertory Theatre, and the author of two books of humour.

OLIVER STALLYBRASS, ex-librarian, ex-publisher, now does a variety of literary and para-literary work which includes editing the *Journal of the Royal Central Asian Society* and acting as U.K. Editorial Representative to Stanford University Press. He has co-authored a chess book and translated novels by Knut Hamsun, Axel Jensen and Rolf Døcker, film scripts by Carl Dreyer and a French history of the Italian cinema. His compilations include a checklist of Forster's writings which formed the starting-point for B. J. Kirkpatrick's *Bibliography*, and 97 pages of index to George Orwell's *Collected Essays, Journalism and Letters*.

GEORGE H. THOMSON is the author of *The Fiction of E. M. Forster* (1967). He was born at Bluevale, Ontario, in 1924, and received the M.A. and Ph.D. degrees from the University of Toronto. Since then he has taught in Canada and the United States. In addition to his interest in Forster, he has written on Thomas Hardy, William Golding and J. R. R. Tolkien. During 1967–8 he held a Canada Council Senior Fellowship.

Index of Forster's Works

Uncollected essays etc. are identified by their number in
B. J. Kirkpatrick's *Bibliography*

General Index